Misunderstanding Terrorism

Misunderstanding Terrorism

Marc Sageman

PENN

UNIVERSITY OF PENNSYLVANIA PRESS

PHILADELPHIA

For my parents, who survived the worst political violence in history

Published by
University of Pennsylvania Press
Philadelphia, Pennsylvania 19104-4112
www.upenn.edu/pennpress

Printed in the United States of America on acid-free paper
10 9 8 7 6 5 4 3 2

Cataloging-in-Publication Data is available from the Library of Congress.

ISBN 978-0-8122-4889-0 hardcover
ISBN 978-0-8122-9371-5 ebook

Contents

Introduction

Since childhood, I've been haunted by the issue of political violence. For me, new political massacres have always raised the question, "How is this possible?" For the past 45 years, I've studied this issue, first from the perspective of the victims and then from that of the perpetrators. In the past decade, I had access to inside information about these perpetrators and was able to interview a few dozen of them. As my understanding grew, I perceived a huge gap between that understanding and the portrayals of terrorism in the media, Internet, and official government statements, which create the conventional wisdom on the subject. Our understanding of terrorism has very important implications for the development of policies to deal with it. Is the threat to our security so great that we should give up some of our fundamental rights such as liberty, free speech, and privacy? Should the state preventively detain, or even kill, a person suspected of being a terrorist? Because of the gravity of these questions, in this book I address what I see as a general misunderstanding of terrorism.

My obsession with political violence comes from the fact that my parents are Holocaust survivors. Like most survivors, they never talked about the war, including the details of their own suffering, least of all with their children, whom they tried to protect at all costs. And like many children of survivors, I never asked them about their experience, to spare them the pain of revisiting their trauma. This tacit conspiracy of silence lasted until I left home for college, where I became obsessed with accounts of other survivors. After spending two years devouring the wealth of information on the Holocaust at Widener Library at Harvard, I did not want that time to have been wasted and wrote my undergraduate thesis on how people psychologically survived concentration camps.

Interested in the physical and social aspects of suffering, I became an MD–PhD training fellow taking my PhD in political sociology. With this background, I focused on tropical medicine, a mixture of medicine and politics. To pursue this interest, following my education I joined the US Navy because it had the best practical training program in this field with hospitals in the tropics. I was stationed in Okinawa, where I became aware of the boat people fleeing Cambodia. The atrocities of the Pol Pot regime made it clear that genocide was not a thing of the past. How was this possible? The United Nations and multiple conventions were established to prevent genocide, yet here was definitely another instance. As the US military was doing nothing to alleviate the suffering of millions of Cambodian victims, I joined the only US government agency that did—which I cannot name for legal reasons.[1]

That agency was doing something about another new genocide. The Soviet Union had invaded Afghanistan, killing about a tenth of its population, externally displacing another third mostly to Pakistan and Iran, and internally displacing another sizable portion. It is in the official record that I was posted to Islamabad the last two years of the Soviet Afghan War and then to New Delhi. In preparation for my trips to the Middle East and beyond, I read extensively about Islam and the history, politics, and sociology of the Middle East and Afghanistan in particular.

Introduction

I resigned in 1991 when the Soviet Union collapsed, and returned to the practice of medicine, specializing in psychiatry. The field had dramatically changed in the previous decade; psychiatrists had agreed upon a common vocabulary to describe mental disorders, and the biological revolution in psychiatry and cognitive revolution in psychology were in full swing. During my psychiatric residency at the University of Pennsylvania, terrorists bombed the World Trade Center in 1993. A *Wall Street Journal* reporter interviewed me as an expert on the Mujahedin and their allies in Islamabad, looking for background information on the attack: the bomber Ramzi Youssef had been trained on the Afghan-Pakistan border. This was the origin of my public role as a commentator on terrorism, which I would take up ten years later in connection with the second, devastating attack on the World Trade Center. In my medical career, my interest in violence led me to specialize in forensic psychiatry, the scientific study of behavior that informs legal issues. This allowed me to interview hundreds of murder defendants for competency to stand trial and evaluation of their criminal responsibility.

In the mid-1990s, I joined the University of Pennsylvania's Solomon Asch Center for the Study of Ethnopolitical Conflict (SACSEC), which brought scholars from various fields, many of whom later became prominent in terrorism research.[2] Inspired by discussions at the center, I explored social movement theory and the literature on gangs and resumed my study of the root causes of the Holocaust. One book caused me to shift my interest from victims to perpetrators: without perpetrators, there are no victims. Christopher Browning published his study on a German Reserve Police Battalion that participated in the *Einsatzgruppen*, the German military mobile units that killed Jews in mass shootings.[3] Contrary to the conventional wisdom, these policemen were not Nazis or young indoctrinated soldiers. Instead, they were older men, mostly married with children, who had joined the police reserves in order to dodge the draft but were sent to the Eastern front, their sole mission to shoot Jews at close range. Before their first mass murder, they were given the choice to opt out of the massacres, but only a handful from the five-hundred strong battalion elected to do so. Browning's explanation of this choice by "ordinary men" was social psychological, based on experiments on conformity, obedience, and social roles. His argument was soon challenged by one based on ideology—namely, that "Hitler's willing executioners" were simply motivated by an "eliminationist anti-Semitism."[4] This debate about how people become violent is constantly repeated in terrorism research under the puzzle of radicalization. Is it a normal social psychological process? Or are they simply fanatic "true believers," brainwashed by a murderous ideology to carry out massacres? I explored these topics by teaching seminars on the social psychology of violence and trauma at the undergraduate and graduate levels.

The 9/11 attacks narrowed my focus. First, I wanted to know who these terrorists were—had I trained them? Probably not, as I had dealt only with Afghans, and there were no Afghans in al Qaeda. I wanted to understand what we knew about these terrorists. I examined their biographies using epidemiological and social scientific methodology to test the validity of Western assumptions about them. I collected information on the people who committed the 9/11 attacks and traced the evolution of their global neojihadi ideology and the emergence of these specific groups of terrorists. At one time I called this wave of terrorism—which includes the perpetrators of the 1993 World Trade Center bombing in New York and of the wave of bombings in Paris in 1995, al Qaeda and its affiliates, and now the Islamic State in Iraq and the Levant or Daesh[5]—the "global Salafi jihad." It is global in its targeting the West (the far enemy) rather than Middle East despots (the near enemy).[6] But it is not Salafi, and mainstream Muslims object to the term "jihad" because jihad is declared by a legitimate government, not by individuals (just like in the West, where only governments declare war), and it is strictly rule bound, protecting noncombatants, women, and children. Perpetrators, however, claim they are doing jihad even though they target innocent noncombatants without sanction from any legitimate government. I therefore call this form of terrorism the global neojihad—not jihad, but like jihad.

Strongly influenced by the works of historians and sociologists applying social movement theory to Islamic movements,[7] I used my 9/11 data to refute our conventional wisdom about terrorists, but the research still left me without a clear understanding of them. Chance meetings with academic colleagues, however, opened new avenues of research. A conversation with Elihu Katz led me to review his work on political influence, positing a two-step process: first, conversion of opinion makers, who then influence the rank and file.[8] Bill Labov suggested studying Rodney Stark's argument that Christianity grew geometrically during its early centuries through conversion of acquaintances.[9] While exploring the sociology of religion, I encountered Bill Bainbridge, one of the readers of my undergraduate thesis, who had gone on to become a legend in the field.[10] From this further research, I learned that the growth of cults, like that of gangs, is based on friendship and kinship, what I call "a bunch of guys." The context is extremely important in this process and had been neglected in the conventional focus on terrorists as individuals rather than members of a group. I wondered whether the path to political violence was a collective journey, not an individual one, even for so-called lone wolves.

Later, continuing my focus on social movements, I encountered social network analysis, a new tool that held some promise in generating counterintuitive insights in group formation and dynamics.[11] But over the next decade, as I collaborated with more than half a dozen teams of cutting-edge mathematicians, I came to see that their calculations were based on flawed databases. Rubbish in, rubbish out. I also realized that my own original database was inaccurate because its basis of news articles was later refuted by other, more reliable information. It is very hard to categorize the complexity of human relationships and capture their dynamics in a static graph even with excellent data. Fleeting ties can have a disproportionate impact, while long-term connections can reflect inertia instead of significance.

In the summer of 2003, I presented my preliminary findings at a National Research Council meeting on terrorism. Phil Zelikow, the executive director of the 9/11 Commission, was so impressed by the empirical basis for my arguments that he invited me to be part of the first panel of experts to present at the Commission. Believing that my sample of just 25 subjects was not large enough for this presentation before a national audience, I scrambled in the next two months to gather enough data for a more respectable sample of 75 terrorists. After the University of Pennsylvania Press approached me with a request to turn my presentation into a book, I further expanded my sample to 172 terrorists and explored potential new insights from social network analysis. The result was my first book, *Understanding Terror Networks*.[12]

Terry Gross, host of National Public Radio's *Fresh Air*, was our neighbor, and my wife asked her whether she would be interested in the book for her program. After she read it, Terry invited me for an interview on *Fresh Air*, which propelled me further into the limelight. To my surprise, my book became a bestseller in the field and I received invitations to participate in many government-sponsored conferences. By late 2004, I was spending several days each week in Washington, and my clinical and forensic practice in Philadelphia was faltering. I was at a turning point: I could not pursue my medical practice and terrorism research at the same time. Terrorism research was a very risky choice, because up to that point, I had done it all on my own without outside funding. With my wife's complete support, I closed down my practice and we moved to Washington, DC, where I started a new life as an independent consultant on national security, terrorism, and political violence.

In early 2005, I had an experience that taught me an important lesson about Russian and American responses to terrorism. The Russian government invited me to be the first expert to testify before the Beslan Commission, formed to investigate the horrible school massacre of the previous year. The State Department encouraged me to go, hoping that it would contribute to better Russian-US relations. When I got to Russia, I was treated like royalty. After giving a few public lectures and meeting with experts and the national academy, I met with the commission. The vice president of the Russian Senate, who was presiding, asked what had made the 9/11 Commission so successful. I told him I had only been a witness, but from my perspective, it was serious about getting to the bottom of the failure to prevent the 9/11 attacks and accordingly granted immunity to government officials. The commissioners whispered among themselves for a few minutes. The vice president finally asked me, "Why should we hold these meetings if we cannot punish anyone?" Obviously, the Beslan Commission was not an attempt to get at the truth, much to the disappointment of the murdered children's families, some of whom I had met. The commissioners had little interest in how or why people became terrorists.

Meanwhile, the Sandia National Laboratory had invited me to spend a summer there with its social network analysis team to generate new insights into the evolution of terrorist networks. This was the start of my collaboration with several technical teams over the next few years, to explore the application of various techniques to terrorism research. Like all the national laboratories, Sandia is filled with very smart people, who try to apply mathematical techniques to real-life problems. Terrorism was now the national security problem *du jour*, but they lacked any background knowledge about it. Despite their brilliance in their field, they showed a great deal of naïveté outside it. For instance, one prominent scientist asked me whether, from reading the Quran, I could derive al Qaeda's strategy and tactics, which would help his team predict its next targets and prevent future attacks! This faith that superior US technological advantage will solve any social problem, just as it does in the physical sciences, occurs throughout the US government, especially in research funding agencies, where engineers are commonly in charge of funding social projects.

My collaboration with scientists and engineers convinced me that, as in medicine, new insights would not spring from sophisticated analysis of thin and unreliable data (basically my own original matrix of 172 al Qaeda terrorists) but from more intense research in real-life situations. This meant field research to reconstruct what led people to turn to political violence. Up to then, it was assumed that the danger to the West came from outside, the Middle East or Afghanistan, from enemy commandos infiltrated into Western countries as in the 9/11 attacks, in which most of the terrorists were Saudis, led by Arab students in Hamburg, who attacked the United States after their training in Afghanistan. My data, however, suggested that the danger was already in the West, from immigrants or second-generation militants, self-organizing into informal "bunches of guys," embedded into a larger network of militants and distributed over areas of Muslim immigration in the West, such as Paris, Hamburg, Montreal, Amsterdam, Madrid, London, and Brussels, where attacks had occurred or would occur. My analysis indicated that London had become the center of the global jihad in the West.[13] The London bombings a year later in 2005 confirmed this analysis. They along with the Madrid bombings showed that, as I suspected,

Introduction

the threat was not from the outside but from global neo-jihadi militants already in the West. As a result of these massacres, understanding the transformation of first- or second-generation Muslim immigrants and Muslim converts into violent perpetrators, a process labeled radicalization, became the most pressing issue in terrorism research. And this called for more intense field research to investigate this transformation.

So in early 2005, I started a three-year collaboration with Scott Atran from the University of Michigan. For a time, we explored together the suburbs of Madrid and Hamburg, the slums of Tangiers and Tetuan in Morocco, and Kurdish areas in Turkey.[14] In 2007, the Air Force Research Laboratory gave me a grant for field research on radicalization and the "specificity" of terrorists in relation to their peers (see chapter 2). Thanks to this support, I conducted fieldwork in poor neighborhoods where Muslims constitute a large minority in Paris, London, Madrid, Hamburg, Berlin, Brussels, Amsterdam, The Hague, Copenhagen, Mombasa, Sydney, Melbourne, and Singapore.[15]

Another turn in my career came in 2006, when the US Secret Service invited me to join its National Threat Assessment Center, which gave me access to the daily stream of intelligence on the threat to the United States and the president. Reading this daily traffic, I realized that the threat to the West was evolving. First, I came to appreciate that there was an Atlantic divide between the threat in Europe and that in the United States. While European Muslims came from refugees or families in search of economic opportunities and were poor, many in the United States came from educated elites—college professors, physicians, engineers—whose children had better opportunities. The danger seemed greater in Europe. Second, it seemed that the social status of militants had degraded, from university students like the Hamburg leaders of the 9/11 attacks in my 2004 sample to hoodlums from poor neighborhoods in the sample I had by 2008. Third, I realized that there were at least four prongs in the process of radicalization: moral outrage at recent political events, a warlike ideology (the West is at war with Islam), personal experiences that resonated with this ideology, and mobilization through existing militant networks. Fourth, I noted that in contrast to the alarmism of American experts based on older data, the threat from al Qaeda Central seemed to have diminished despite some rare operations in Europe. I noted the greater role of the Internet in neojihadi communication. In my second book, *Leaderless Jihad*,[16] I argued that radicalization in the West was a largely autonomous process that would continue but that its environment had changed. Aggressive counterterrorism measures worldwide now prevented face-to-face interactions among potential terrorists and forced them to meet and communicate on the Internet, resulting in a leaderless jihad, orchestrated online.[17] This had strong implications for counterterrorism strategy and policy. If my argument was correct, the threat was already in the West, from self-radicalizing militants, and not from the outside through infiltration of foreign militants, resulting in an increase in homegrown attacks, disconnected from foreign terrorist organizations.

Although the book gathered very positive reviews in the academic community, a review in *Foreign Affairs* distorted my process-based argument in an insulting review and accused me of writing that al Qaeda Central was finished. This alarmist review claimed that homegrown terrorism was a myth and that al Qaeda was on the move and not on the run because of the London bombings three years earlier.[18] A *New York Times* article distorted this dispute over a process into one over two exclusive ideal-types of terrorism: a leaderless one, emerging spontaneously from the bottom up, and a leader-led one, deliberately planned from the top down. Very few of my colleagues in the intelligence community, I discovered, had actually read my book; they had read only the review's mischaracterization of my argument. Instead of either of the exclusive positions, they adopted a middle one, where both types of terrorism, top down and bottom up, existed, and they did not realize that this was precisely my argument, based on process rather than ideal types. Aggressive counterterrorism and the Internet had shifted the global neojihad in the West into more of a leaderless one.

At this time, the New York Police Department, whose commissioners had read the book and completely agreed with it, invited me to become its first scholar in residence to help the department protect the city. I worked closely with Mitch Silber, the director of the NYPD Intelligence Analysis Unit, and monitored the threat in New York City.[19] After a few months, I noticed that the threat was even less organized and more fluid than I had previously appreciated: militants imagined that they were part of a large global neojihadi community linking them all together. People moved in and out of this community, which had no clear boundaries and no formal structure. I compared it to a social blob, since I had no better term to describe this ever-changing group. Most of the participants of this community were talkers and not doers, but on rare occasions someone emerged from this community to try to carry out a violent attack. It was difficult to predict which one was an actual danger, and the NYPD was having trouble monitoring all these potential terrorists because of their numbers.

Overseas, NYPD detectives helped me in my fieldwork in Europe, and some introduced me to their local counterparts. My findings confirmed the "blob theory"—that terrorists mostly emerged from this loose, fluid, and amorphous political protest community. I shared my findings with local law enforcement agencies. In Copenhagen I attended a presentation by the domestic intelligence service that used my term, "social blob," for the neojihadi threat in Denmark. When asked, the presenter said they could not come up with a better term and so adopted mine.

Supplementing my field research and interviews of former violent militants abroad, I collected trial records of those in prison. Unlike defendants in the United States, those in European courts must answer questions of prosecutors or judges. This constitutes an invaluable primary source, albeit quite biased, about their path to political violence. However, privacy laws are much stronger in Europe than the United States, and trial transcripts are not available to the public. Much of my time in Europe consisted of developing relationships among lawyers, prosecutors, and security agencies. In an implicit quid pro quo, I briefed them on my research, and they often gave me access to their records.

In November 2009, the US Army Deputy Chief of Staff for Intelligence called me after the Fort Hood massacre by

Major Nidal Hasan. After I met with the general, he invited me to join Army Counter-Intelligence and Counter-Terrorism to assess and identify the insider threat in the Army. Some senators and congressmen claimed that the Army was infiltrated by Muslim militants, threatening it from the inside. The chair of the House Committee on Homeland Security claimed that the FBI had already opened more than one hundred terrorism investigations on Muslim soldiers. I was given carte blanche to investigate any soldier or civilian in the Army to assess the situation. I resumed reading the daily top-secret stream of intelligence to monitor the threat to the United States, the West, and specifically the Army. After reviewing all the Army investigation files and the court-martial records, I examined the evidence of relevant FBI Joint Terrorism Task Forces on suspected Army personnel.

After a two-year investigation, I had discovered only four cases of Islamist threat to the Army in the previous decade: Sergeant Hasan Akbar, the perpetrator of a fragging (killing a fellow soldier with a fragmentation grenade) incident in Kuwait in 2003; Specialist Ryan Anderson, a convert who had volunteered to spy for al Qaeda in 2004; Major Nidal Hasan; and Specialist Naser Abdo, who tried a copycat Fort Hood attack in 2011. They were all disgruntled loners, Muslims, but not Salafi extremists, and two had prominent symptoms of mental illness. The wars against Muslims had transformed their dual American-Muslim loyalty into a divided loyalty, American versus Muslim. Imminent negative change in status, such as impending discharge, detention, or unwanted deployment abroad catalyzed their anger into action before it was too late. In an army of about 1.1 million people (in uniform and civilian), this amounted to about four cases per million over ten years, giving it a very low base rate of 4 per 10,000,000 per year. Such rates are usually given per 100,000 people per year: the insider threat to the army was 0.04 per 100,000 per year. In addition, there was no indication of penetration or outside direction from any enemy for the four cases. In fact, I argued that any real attempt to turn the army inside out to ferret out the alleged insider threat would institute a culture of paranoia. This would in essence break down the army, whose effectiveness is based on small unit loyalty. Without this trust at the squad level, the army would destroy itself. It was therefore important not to overreact. A good way to prevent such a threat is to bring disgruntled loners back into the fold through good leadership by engaging them more in unit activities. The concept is simple: one does not betray one's buddies.

I briefed the House Committee on Homeland Security staff twice on my findings, each time for two hours. Obviously, this was not what its chair wanted to hear, and the committee ignored the empirical evidence that might interfere with his fear-mongering strategy to enhance his political standing. He later held a full House hearing on the significant insider threat in the Army despite my findings. To me, this was an important lesson about the lack of integrity of some politicians, who amplify the threat of terrorism for their own political gains and mislead the public into misunderstanding terrorism.

With no terrorist threat to investigate, the Army expanded my mission into understanding spies, who also constitute an insider threat. I spent the next year reviewing the voluminous top-secret files on the 40 army spies since World War II to develop a model of the process leading some people to betray their country and organization.

The next phase of my career came in 2012. That summer, in Afghanistan, there was an escalation of "green on blue" violence: Afghan allies in uniform (green depicts allies in war games) were shooting and killing International Security Assistance Forces (ISAF; our coalition, as blue is the color of one's own troops). The French, who had suffered some of the most murderous attacks, pulled out of the coalition and returned home saying they had not come to Afghanistan in order to be killed by those they were supposed to help. The increased number of attacks was threatening to further split the coalition, as the war was especially unpopular among our allies. The ISAF Deputy Chief of Staff for Intelligence invited me to come to Kabul and help with what had been just relabeled the insider threat to ISAF.

In mid-October I arrived at ISAF headquarters, where I found little information available about these attacks and no clue as to where the information might be. (I later discovered that ISAF Joint Command [IJC] intelligence, which was in charge of analyzing these attacks, had created a matrix of factors leading to these attacks, but refused to share it with people outside its unit.) IJC intelligence believed that the attacks were the product of a cultural misunderstanding between ISAF and Afghan troops that had escalated in the field into shooting matches, resulting in the killing of ISAF troops. IJC had found that only 18 percent of the attacks had any link to the Afghan resistance, supporting its cultural thesis.

Unaware of the existence of the IJC matrix, I gathered information on the attacks through a network of military friends, who facilitated my access to army legal investigations into each attack. I cajoled Marine Corps lawyers in Afghanistan to share the results of their own investigations. I got the full cooperation of the French, due to my friendship with their commanding officer, and the British, who had been victims of most of the summer's attacks resulting in public demands that its soldiers come home. The Ministry of Defense did not want to abandon ISAF and gave me permission to interview perpetrators in British custody. The Afghan government also gave me access to the shooters in its custody. The ISAF headquarters counterintelligence unit, where I was lodged, helped me examine all the electronic evidence.

After two months of intensive investigation, I realized that none of the attacks in 2012 followed the thesis of cultural insensitivity escalating into lethality. In fact, almost all the 49 attacks in 2012 had been premeditated, especially during the month of Ramadan (July 20 to August 20 of that year), and 57 percent had definite links with local insurgents, while another 18 percent had probable or possible links with them. About 25 percent had no links to the insurgency and were the result of mental illness, drug abuse, corruption, or rage at a personal insult. The vast majority of perpetrators had come to the Afghan military without any terrorist leanings and changed after joining. All the attacks involved strangers shooting at strangers (there was no previous contact that could have led to cultural misunderstanding) and in most attacks, the shooters' Afghan peers had known about their plans to carry out an attack.

These findings were of course the opposite of what IJC had argued all along. I shared my data with IJC, which immediately upgraded the percentage of links to the insurgency to 48 percent but still strongly disputed my findings. It ordered me to confine myself to concepts in the ISAF standard operating procedures (SOP) despite the fact that they did not fit the reality we were dealing with. For instance, many of the perpetrators were volunteers for the jihad: they were not recruited or infiltrated into Afghan forces. According to IJC, volunteers came under the category "unknown," which made the cultural thesis plausible, even though we knew this was not true. Such catch-22 reasoning is not unusual in the military. I responded that if the SOP categories did not reflect reality, we had to change them. Given the importance of this issue for the ISAF alliance and the fact that real lives were at stake, an independent panel of intelligence experts was immediately convened to resolve this dispute between IJC and me. The panel completely agreed with my findings since the data spoke for itself and IJC had relied on unsubstantiated claims and its need to conform to irrelevant SOP. ISAF changed its SOP and implemented measures I recommended. Green-on-blue violence was dramatically reduced after these measures were instituted. This is one of my proudest achievements: it saved American and allied lives. My contract with the Army expired three months later, and I was finally completely out of government service.

My work in the government and in the field had provided me with a wealth of data that I had not had the opportunity to analyze. I needed some distance from my operational activities to frame them and construct a model of the turn to political violence. I went back to the literature on social science methodology, gangs, cults, social psychology, social movements, and political violence to gather insights into this process.

Meanwhile, because of my earlier work in criminal defense and my research on terrorism, lawyers on terrorism cases started to call me to help them as an expert witness for the defense. This gave me access to mountains of evidence in the discovery material, including transcripts of interviews with terrorists sometimes amounting to more than five thousand pages as well as their electronic communications over several years. Many of these cases included hundreds of hours of taped conversations before their arrests. More important, it also gave me access to the defendants themselves, whom I could interview over days in prison. However, as with classified information, I had to sign an agreement not to share this wealth of material with anyone not connected to the case.

Since I cannot use US classified material and court material, I collected reliable and detailed information on political violent perpetrators elsewhere, including trial transcripts and documents from cases in which I was not involved. These included trials in the United States, Britain, and the Netherlands; long court judgments for more than a dozen trials in France; interrogations of suspects in France and Belgium; and trial notes in Germany, Britain, and Spain. I have also gone to terrorist trials in Spain, Denmark, Britain, and the United States, where I took notes. When I compare what I read in the newspapers or in academic journals about the cases in which I had personally been involved with the primary sources, I noted that the reporting was significantly flawed, with the exception of very few investigators, who had spent years on just one case.[20] Most of the reporting on terrorism in the United States comes from politically motivated leaks from secondary sources, intelligence officials, or politicians superficially briefed on these cases. The articles are often datelined Washington, DC, and not from the field, where the investigations took place.

Over the years, I have interviewed dozens of global neojihadi terrorists in Afghan, Saudi, and federal US prisons (including Guantanamo Bay), in addition to released former terrorists and close relatives and friends of convicted or killed terrorists on five continents. There is no substitute for access to the defendants, who are the only ones with a privileged window into their motivations and their paths to violence. In regard to Daesh, the State Department invited me to spend two weeks in Baghdad in 2014, talking to government officials and young Iraqis about Daesh and political violence in their country. The view from the field bore almost no relationship to the hysterical press accounts in the United States. The European press was a little more responsible in its reporting; what passes for US investigative journalism in terrorism is simply a few superficial searches on the Internet, publication of politically motivated leaks from anonymous sources, and quick phone calls to so-called terrorism experts. Few newspapers have learned the painful lessons of the flawed reporting in the frantic rush to war in Iraq in 2002–3, when front-page stories of the most respectable American newspapers frequently announced new evidence for weapons of mass destruction or links between Iraq and al Qaeda, which turned out to be nonexistent.

In 2014, I published a controversial paper on the cause of stagnation in terrorism research. Although the government funds academics trained in social science methodology to analyze data, it does not share any information on terrorist operations with them. On the other hand, in-house government analysts, who have access to most classified information,[21] lack the sophisticated methodological background to fully and accurately analyze their data. In technical terms, they generally do not understand the importance of control groups, representativeness of a sample, the sensitivity and specificity of any instrument, or Bayesian probability, as we shall see in chapter 2. I concluded, drawing the flaws of this situation to their extreme, that academics understand everything but know nothing, while government analysts know everything but understand nothing.

Government analysts are also hindered by politics. They must include people convicted in FBI sting operations as true terrorists, while the evidence indicates that, but for the FBI informant or undercover agent, they would never have turned violent. Furthermore, these analysts must mix apples and oranges: people convicted for a violent offense are mixed in with people who sent a small amount of money to terrorist front organizations and with people who want to fight abroad but would never carry out a terrorist operation at home. The result is a great inflation of the terrorist threat to the United States, resulting in popular hysteria that leads to calls to abrogate civil liberties of suspect populations and demands to kill hundreds or thousands of innocent Muslims abroad. European countries have a much more measured reaction to a much greater global neojihadi threat—as their Muslim population is much greater than in the United States, closer to the combat zone (some even rent cars to travel back and forth to Syria), and more likely to carry out global neojihadi attacks.

The US government had a failure of imagination that contributed to the tragedy of 9/11. Usually, governments learn from their mistakes and try to make sure they never repeat them. The US government learned that lesson— but now the pendulum has swung the other way: the US government is suffering from an excess of imagination on terrorism, leading it to curtail our civil liberties without gaining much in national security. Trying to prevent a repeat of 9/11, it has again and again let its imagination run wild and responds to worst-case scenarios without objectively assessing the real threat. And when there is not enough evidence to arrest someone, legions of confidential informants or undercover agents set up credulous suspects in sting operations. The arrests and convictions of these people who are then labeled terrorists feed a vicious cycle: the convictions are taken as proof that this inflated threat to national security exists, which leads to the search of ever more suspects in a self-fulfilling prophecy, a process that soldiers call a "self-licking ice-cream." This book tries to break this cycle by bringing realistic numbers into the assessment of the threat facing the West. I then describe the process of turning to political violence and show how a misunderstanding of terrorism in the West has dramatically inflated fear of the actual danger posed by neojihadis and led to overreaction of the counterterrorist community, threatening fundamental civil liberties. In closing, I recommend straightforward policies that will end this threat instead of perpetuating it.

The Actual Threat

When al Qaeda–linked terrorists hijacked four airplanes and crashed two into the World Trade Center, one into the Pentagon, and one in the Pennsylvania countryside on the morning of September 11, 2001, it was beyond belief and understanding. People stared, in fascination and horror, at television images of the planes approaching and crashing into the World Trade Center, the smoking towers, and their eventual collapse. Hijackings of airliners had been occurring for several decades, and terrorist acts related to the Middle East for years, but these were different. The sheer number of people killed and wounded, as well as the enormous destruction and damage to property, set them apart. These attacks, with their chilling perpetrators bent on suicide and mass murder, were entirely alien to our mental universe.

The 9/11 attacks changed the psyche of people not just in America but throughout the Western world. Fear spread into their daily lives, leading to screening not just at airports but also at sporting events and concerts; and in the wake of terrorist incidents or threats, people canceled plans to travel to affected regions. It also led to anti-Muslim sentiment and actions, as Westerners blamed an entire community for the actions of a very small number and suspected innocent people of being likely terrorists.

That fear led to restrictions on civil liberties, as governments curbed rights in their zeal to prevent further attacks. In the United States, Congress overwhelmingly passed the Patriot Act without the usual discussions regarding the provisions of such a major law. Likewise, Britain passed the Prevention of Terrorism Act in 2005 despite strong criticism by human rights organizations. France allowed long periods of a state of siege, suspending common civil rights after major terrorist attacks. Canada and Australia passed controversial antiterrorist legislation in response to the 9/11 attacks. Outside the West, this change of attitude allowed authoritarian governments to eliminate domestic dissent without much Western protest by labeling their opposition "terrorism."

This changed environment leads naturally to the question of just how serious was the global neojihadi threat to the West, the threat emanating from organizations like al Qaeda or from people claiming to act on their behalf, in the post-9/11 decade. The scope of that threat has been debated, with the "clash of civilization" argument going as far as suggesting that it was an existential threat to the West. Views about the nature of this threat are also divided: a top-down threat of foreign terrorist organizations infiltrating and attacking the West or one more bottom-up, with homegrown militants turning to violence, sometimes with the help of foreign organizations. Since the number of global neojihadi plots or attacks, successful and failed, during that decade is limited, we can in fact examine all of them to settle these debates.

Inclusion Criteria for the Survey of Global Neojihadi Plots/Attacks in the West

To determine what plots to study for this assessment (listed in table 1), I used several criteria. First, since it takes time for reliable information to surface about any attack, I am limiting this survey to the period from September 11, 2001 to September 10, 2011. Second, I require these plots/ attacks to be in the West: any plot not reaching the West is not included. By the West, I mean the European Union, North America, and Australia/New Zealand. Third, the plots/attacks must belong to the global neojihadi wave of violence and include those linked to al Qaeda and its allies and homegrown incidents carried out in the name of the global neojihad.[1]

Fourth, and most important, inclusion into this survey requires serious attempts at violence. Many young Muslims talk in very violent terms and even discuss carrying out attacks when venting their frustration, but these utterances are often no more than youthful bragging and rarely lead to anything more than just words. For inclusion, there needs to be some actual danger to the public beyond fantasizing, indicated by acts to further the plot, such as acquiring weapons or the components of bombs, casing targets, or recording martyrdom videos. The survey includes both attacks that have been carried out, whether successful or not, and serious plots that did not reach completion despite clear acts in furtherance of the plan. Idle campfire chats to kill the boredom of Waziristan evenings[2] or wishful thinking about plots that never went beyond the stage of just imagination or talk have not been included.[3] In addition, as noted, this survey is limited to actual violent acts and therefore does not include forms of material support such as providing money, shelter, equipment, or translation in support of foreign terrorist organizations.

Fifth, neojihadis must initiate and carry out these attacks without encouragement or help from government agents. European intelligence officers tease me that there is such a small danger in the United States, that the FBI manufactures terrorists through sting operations.[4] Europeans do not carry out sting operations, which they consider outright provocation and incompatible with liberal democracy. Many US intelligence analysts, however, believe that targets of sting operations were rightfully arrested and convicted before they had a chance to carry out a terrorist operation. I return to this issue, but all too often, these state agents became "entrepreneurial" agents provocateurs "subtly coaxing radicalized but hesitant individuals into action. Even without providing overt encouragement, the informant often plays the role of an enabler, offering people with extreme views but faint hearts the means to act, thereby potentially facilitating actions that otherwise might not occur."[5] In all such cases that I reviewed, the defendants posed no real threat of violence because they had no capability or realistic hope of carrying out an attack. State agents made all the obstacles in the way of carrying out attacks disappear and supplied weapons to these helpless militants, who posed no danger to the public. I therefore excluded sting operations from the survey.

Finally, there must be some link to the global neojihad through interaction with other global neojihadis or at least accessing their websites. This last criterion attempts to eliminate crimes committed not for political reasons but because of mental disorder. Mass murderers suffering from mental disorders often carry out their killings for an ideology. For instance, fired postal worker Joseph M. Harris, dressed in a ninja outfit, killed four colleagues in October 1991 in New Jersey, giving rise to the expression "going postal." He explained to me that he did so for the civil rights movement and considered himself a political prisoner, but he had never been part of this movement or even interacted with any of its participants.[6] This type of case is simply mass murder, and its inclusion would not shed any light on political violence but would distract us from discovering the dynamics that might lead to such violence. Therefore, I have excluded cases like Naveed Haq's shooting spree in July 2006, shortly after Haq's release from a mental hospital.[7] Both Harris and Haq suffered from severe mental disorders that affected their thinking and significantly contributed to their respective crimes. Neither was connected to a political protest community that might have given meaning to their senseless crimes.

This does not mean that anyone suffering from mental disorder should be excluded from this survey, which includes several attacks carried out by people with severe mental disorders, like the failed bombing in Exeter; the Santa Barbara, Italy, barracks attack; and the Copenhagen Hotel bombing (incidents 42, 50, and 58 in table 1). This is of course a judgment call, but the people included in the survey were in contact with other global neojihadis, who supported their beliefs, and their violent ideas were not just locked inside their minds. Despite their disorder, they formulated and carried out attacks that were consistent with the shared beliefs of their community. It is this sharing that distinguishes them from those excluded from the survey.

Survey of Global Neojihadi
Post-9/11 Plots in the West

To construct the survey, I compiled a database of all global neojihadi incidents in the West since 9/11 through review of both open and classified sources (all of them were reported in the press). I traced these incidents through their conclusion in litigation; much of the initial reporting was sensational and full of errors (see introduction). These errors were rarely retracted later, but court proceedings provided information that is more reliable. Some suspects arrested with much fanfare on charges found to be without foundation were later quietly released. In other cases, when there was enough evidence to support a trial, information from the proceedings refuted the original claims.[8] For instance, Jose Padilla was arrested and accused of plotting a radiological bomb attack ("dirty bomb") in the United States. He was convicted of conspiracy to murder, kidnap, and maim people *overseas*, excluding him from the survey.

After checking the list for completeness with colleagues in both US and foreign governments and in academia, I compared it with other surveys and investigated all their incidents not on my original list for possible inclusion according to my criteria. These surveys varied in quality and differed in conclusions.[9] Some included all the FBI sting operations in their survey and used their inflated number to claim, as one put it, "Al Qaeda and its . . . allies arguably have been able to accomplish the unthinkable—establish at least an embryonic terrorist recruitment, radicalization, and operational structure in the United States."[10] A more nuanced summary of American cases noted that most of them "could be described as more aspirational than operational" and found "no sustained jihadist terrorist campaign in the United States."[11] Clearly, therefore, many of the incidents in these surveys did not meet my inclusion criteria.

The 66 global neojihadi plots or attacks in the West during the post-9/11 decade involved 220 individuals, averaging about 3.3 terrorists per plot. The numbers in the perpetrators column reflect those convicted for directly participating in violence and not simply providing support, matching my criterion. This is a judgment call, and the numbers are approximate, but I think they are close to the real number of people directly participating in violence. I relied on the legal proceedings for each case when I could to arrive at final numbers. For instance, in the Nova investigation (incident 20), of the 44 people arrested, 30 were charged and put on trial, 20 of whom were convicted. Six months later, the Spanish Supreme Court acquitted 15 of them, asserting that no one should be convicted for his ideas—only acts count. Thus the entire legal process reduced the number participating in the Nova plot from 44 to five.

Timeline Distribution of Global Neojihadi Plots/Attacks in the West

Threats vary in their intensity over time. To determine their overall trend, I traced the timeline distribution of these incidents over the post-9/11 decade.

Table 1. Global Neojihadi Post-9/11 Plots in the West

#	Incident	Major suspects	Operation	Country	Date	Link	Perps
1	9/11 Attack on the US	Atta et al.		US	9/11/01	AQ	23
2	Paris US Embassy Plot	Beghal et al.		France	9/13/01	AQ	5
3	Kleine Brogel USAF Plot	Trabelsi et al.		Belgium	9/13/01	AQ	3
4	Concorde Temple Explosion	Domenico Quaranta		Italy	11/4/01	Loner	1
5	Shoe Bomb Airliner Attack	Reid/Badat		UK	12/11/01	AQ	2
6	Sicily Agrigento Prison Fire	Quaranta		Italy	2/14/02	Loner	1
7	Sicily Agrigento Church Fire	Quaranta		Italy	2/26/02	Loner	1
8	Al-Tawhid Plot	Abu Dhess et al.		Germany	4/1/02	Tawhid	5
9	Milan Subway Blast	Quaranta		Italy	5/11/02	Loner	1
10	Heidelberg Plot	Osman Petmezci		Germany	9/5/02	Loner	1
11	Paris Russian Embassy Plot	Benchellali et al.	"Chechen"	France	12/17/02	Ind.	4
12	Wood Green "Ricin" Plot	Kamel Bourgass		UK	1/5/03	Loner	1
13	Sydney Plot	Brigitte/Lodhi		Australia	10/9/03	LeT	2
14	Madrid Train Bombings	Fakhet/Ahmidan		Spain	3/11/04	Ind.	14
15	Fertilizer Bomb Plot	Khyam/Khawaja	Crevice	UK	3/30/04	AQ	6
16	Toledo AVE Train Attack	Ahmidan et al.		Spain	4/2/04	Ind.	?

#	Incident	Major suspects	Operation	Country	Date	Link	Perps
17	Plots v. Various Targets	Azzouz et al.	Hofstad	Netherlands	6/30/04	Ind.	3
18	UK Gas Limo Project	Barot et al.	Rhyme	UK	8/2/04	AQ	8
19	Rotterdam Plot	Yehya Kadouri		Netherlands	9/27/04	Loner	1
20	Plots v. Supreme Court et al.	Achraf et al.	Nova	Spain	10/20/04	Ind.	5
21	Murder of Theo van Gogh	Mohd Bouyeri	Hofstad	Netherlands	11/2/04	Loner	1
22	Allawi Assassination Plot	Rashid et al.		Germany	12/3/04	Ansar	3
23	Plots v. Hirsi Ali et al.	El-Fatmi et al.	Piranha	Netherlands	6/22/05	Ind.	3
24	JIS Plot, Torrence, CA	James et al.		US	7/5/05	Ind.	4
25	London Bombings	MSK et al.	Theseus	UK	7/7/05	AQ	4
26	Failed London Bombings	Ibrahim et al.	Vivace	UK	7/21/05	AQ	6
27	Plot v. AIVD and Politicians	Azzouz et al.	Piranha	Netherlands	10/14/05	Ind.	5
28	Sarajevo Bomb Plot	Bektasevic et al.	Glostrup	Denmark	10/19/05	Ind.	3
29	Melbourne/Sydney Plots	Benbrika et al.	Pendennis	Australia	11/4/05	Ind.	14
30	Toronto-18	Amara et al.	Osage	Canada	6/3/06	Ind.	6
31	Train Suitcase Attack	Hajdib/Hamad		Germany	7/31/06	Ind.	2
32	Liquid Bomb Airliners Plot	Ali et al.	Overt	UK	8/10/06	AQ	9
33	Odense Plot	Zaher/Khaldahi	Vollsmose	Denmark	9/4/06	Ind.	3
34	Oslo Synagogue Plot	Bhatti et al.		Norway	9/21/06	Ind.	2
35	Birmingham Plot	Parviz Khan	Gamble	UK	1/31/07	Ind.	1

Table 1. Global Neojihadi Post-9/11 Plots in the West (*continued*)

#	Incident	Major suspects	Operation	Country	Date	Link	Perps
36	Nancy Multiple Bomb Plots	Kamel Bouchentouf		France	5/2/07	Loner	1
37	London/Glasgow Attacks	Abdulla/Ahmed	Seagram	UK	6/30/07	Ind.	2
38	Copenhagen Bomb Plot	Khürshid/Tokhi	Glasvej	Denmark	9/4/07	AQ	2
39	Sauerland Plot	Gelowicz et al.	Alberich	Germany	9/4/07	IJU	4
40	Barcelona Metro Bomb Plot	Mirza et al.		Spain	1/19/08	TTP	11
41	Bristol Bomb Plot	Isa Ibrahim		UK	4/17/08	Loner	1
42	Exeter Failed Bombing	Nicky Reilly		UK	5/22/08	Loner	1
43	Derby Plot	Krenar Lusha		UK	8/26/08	Loner	1
44	DCRI Bomb Plot	Rany Arnaud et al.		France	12/16/08	Ind.	3
45	Manchester Plot	Abid Naseer et al.	Pathway	UK	4/8/09	AQ	4
46	Little Rock, AR, Shooting	Muhammad/Bledsoe		US	6/1/09	Loner	1
47	Quantico Plot	Boyd et al.		US	7/27/09	Ind.	2
48	Holsworthy Barracks Plot	Fattal/Aweys/Sayed	Neath	Australia	8/4/09	Ind.	3
49	NYC Subway Plot	Zazi et al.	Highrise	US	9/9/09	AQ	3
50	Santa Barbara Barracks Attack	Game/Kol		Italy	10/12/09	Ind.	2
51	US *Jyllands Posten* Plot	David Headley		US	10/27/09	AQ	1
52	Ft. Hood Shooting	Nidal Malik Hasan		US	11/5/09	Loner	1

#	Incident	Major suspects	Operation	Country	Date	Link	Perps
53	Christmas Underwear Bomber	Abdulmutallab		UK/US	12/25/09	AQAP	3
54	Axe Attack v. Cartoonist	Muhidin Gelle		Denmark	1/1/10	Loner	1
55	Failed Times Square Bombing	Faisal Shahzad		US	5/1/10	TTP	1
56	Stabbing of MP Timms	Roshonara Choudhry		UK	5/16/10	Loner	1
57	Oslo Bombing Plot	Davud/Bujak		Norway	7/8/10	AQ	3
58	Copenhagen Hotel Bombing	Lors Doukaev		Belgium	9/10/10	Loner	1
59	Cargo Plane Bomb Attack	Ibrahim al Asiri		UK/US	10/29/10	AQAP	3
60	Stockholm Suicide Bomber	Taimour al-Abdaly		UK/Sweden	12/11/10	Loner	1
61	London Stock Exchange Plot	Chowdhury et al.	Guava	UK	12/20/10	Ind.	4
62	Swedish *Jyllands Posten* Plot	Zalouti et al.	Aqua	Sweden	12/29/10	AQ	4
63	Frankfurt Airport Shooting	Arid Uka		Germany	3/2/11	Loner	1
64	Dusseldorf Bomb Plot	El Kebir et al.		Germany	4/29/11	AQ	4
65	Oldham Couple Terrorists	Mohd and Shasta Khan		UK	7/24/11	Ind.	2
66	Ft. Hood Redux Plot	Naser Abdo		US	7/27/11	Loner	1

Abbreviations: Ansar, al Ansar al Islam; AQ, al Qaeda; AQAP, al Qaeda in the Arabian Peninsula; LeT, Lashkar e-Toiba; IJU, Islamic Jihad Union; Tawhid, al Tawhid wa'l Hijra; TTP, Tarik e-Taliban e-Pakistan.

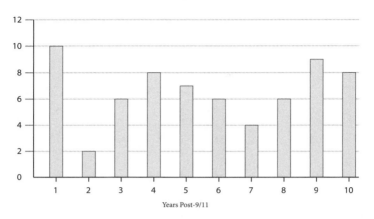

Figure 1. Plots/Attacks in the Ten Years Post-9/11

In each of the six graphs in this chapter, the numbers on horizontal axis indicate years following 9/11. Year 1: September 11, 2001–September 10, 2002; Year 2: September 11, 2002–September 10, 2003, and so on to Year 10: September 11, 2010–September 10, 2011. Figure 1 shows three peaks in the number of these incidents in the decade. The first one occurred in the first year after 9/11 and consisted mostly of attacks planned before 9/11. The sharp decline after this first year shows that the invasion of Afghanistan clearly disrupted al Qaeda's ability to attack the West. A second one occurred from September 2004 to September 2006, corresponding to the period of the most intensive fighting in Iraq, and slowly faded afterward. A third peak emerged in the fall of 2009, after publication of the Muhammad cartoons, the intensification of fighting in Afghanistan, and the emergence of new global neojihadi organizations. This third peak raises the possibility that the threat was increasing at the end of the decade.[12]

If this threat did increase at the end of the decade, we would expect to see more participating global neojihadis at that time. To test whether this did in fact occur, consider a timeline distribution of people involved rather than the incidents.

Figure 2 shows only two peaks in the number of people involved. The first one came in the months after 9/11. This peak includes the 23 people involved in the 9/11 attack, who constitute a majority of the global neojihadis of that year. If we remove them from the timeline, then there were only 17 global neojihadis—a little less than the yearly average. The second peak, from March 2004 through September 2006, was the zenith of the post-9/11 global neojihadi threat to the West. The last five years of the decade show a plateau of about 15 new global neojihadis per year, less than the average of 22 for the whole decade, contradicting the apparent alarming trend of the previous graph. The difference between the two graphs reflects a change in the nature of the incidents. September 10, 2006, marks

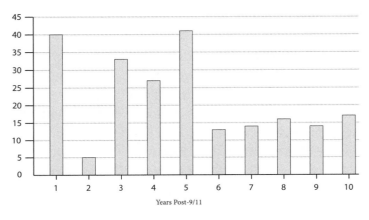

Figure 2. Global Neojihadis in the Ten Years Post-9/11

the halfway point in the decade, and the number of plots divides evenly into 33 plots/attacks for each half. The first half, though, involved 146 terrorists, while the second involved only 74 terrorists. So the number of participants in each incident went from about 4.4 in the first half to about 2.2 in the second, when the threat consisted of "tiny conspiracies, lone gunmen, [and] one-off attacks rather than sustained terrorist campaigns."[13] To further appreciate the significance of this change between the two halves, we need to break down the incidents according to their sponsoring terrorist organizations, if any.

Al Qaeda Plots/Attacks in the West

Not every global neojihadi plot or attack is an "al Qaeda plot," as the press and politicians often call them. However, even those directly linked to al Qaeda vary in al Qaeda's level of involvement—what has been called their "al Qaeda factor"[14]—ranging from direct command and control to provision of training or skill, material support in financing or weapons, or simple endorsement. These variations are important. Lack of al Qaeda direction due to severed communication resulted in failure despite extensive training in the copycat failed London bombing attack (incident 26). In cases of simple endorsement, like the Crevice case (incident 15), arrests of the conspirators put an end to the attack, which was initiated, planned, and executed by the conspirators themselves.[15] By contrast, in centrally directed attacks from abroad like 9/11, the elimination of some conspirators did not stop the operation: when several of the initial 9/11 participants of Yemeni origin could not get visas to come to the United States, they were promptly replaced by Saudis able to get these visas. Like most analysts, I lumped together all the plots/ attacks involving participants with any direct personal contact with any member of al Qaeda about the plot[16] as "al Qaeda plots" for simplicity's sake. These 16 incidents amounted to 25 percent of the total global neojihadi incidents in the West; they involved 87 individuals, which amounts to an average of 5.4 terrorists per al Qaeda incident in contrast to 2.6 per non–al Qaeda incident. This doubling of individuals per al Qaeda plot/attack over the rest of the incidents suggests that these plots were more sophisticated than the others.

To further determine the trend of al Qaeda plots/attacks in the West, figure 3 shows three waves of those attacks. We could interpret the last wave to suggest a resurgence of al Qaeda's ability to project violence into the West on the same level it did in the first two waves, which included 9/11 and the London bombings, respectively. To check this

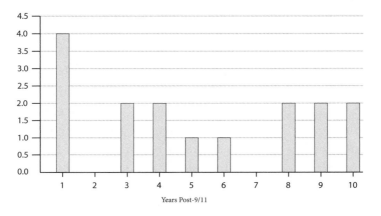

Figure 3. Al Qaeda Plots/Attacks in the Ten Years Post-9/11

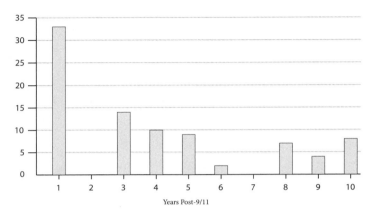

Figure 4. Operational al Qaeda Terrorists in the Ten Years Post-9/11

hypothesis, I constructed a timeline around individuals rather than incidents.

Figure 4 represents the yearly number of operational al Qaeda terrorists in the West—that is, those directly involved in serious plots or attacks. They do not constitute all people linked to al Qaeda arrested in the West, because some were arrested just for belonging to al Qaeda.[17] These latter individuals were active in al Qaeda at the time of their arrest, but they were not involved in any sufficiently serious violent act to be included in the survey.

The first wave of al Qaeda attacks against the West consisted of the 9/11 attacks, two plots in France and Belgium, respectively, and the airline shoe bombs attacks and lasted from September to December 2001. They origi-nated during the time al Qaeda benefited from Taliban protection and sanctuary, allowing it to plan at leisure. The 9/11 attacks, the most devastating al Qaeda opera-tion, were extensively described by the 9/11 Commission and investigative reports.[18] The two plots in France and

Belgium arose from a network of North African immigrants to these countries who had become radicalized in France, Belgium, and England, and then went to Afghanistan, where they trained with al Qaeda before returning to Europe.[19] The shoe bomb airliner attack came from two British militants who joined al Qaeda in Afghanistan and were sent home to carry out attacks on planes bound for the United States. One dropped out; the other carried on but failed when alert fellow passengers and airline attendants subdued him.[20]

The fall 2001 US invasion of Afghanistan eliminated both sanctuary and Taliban support for al Qaeda, wreaked chaos in the organization, and disrupted further attacks in the West, as shown in the two-and-a-half year gap in incidents in the West. The next wave consisted of five al Qaeda plots/attacks in Britain, involving 33 terrorists (6.6 individuals per attack). Although al Qaeda was notified about the first plot, Operation Crevice, after the fact,[21] I still count it in this section. The second plot, Rhyme, was a detailed plan by a longtime al Qaeda member to carry out operations in Britain.[22] British experts called the plot "superficially attractive, but in fact amateurish,"[23] and the FBI concurred that it was "unlikely to be as successful as described . . . while ambitious and creative, [it was] far-fetched."[24]

The last three attacks in this second wave were connected to an al Qaeda intermediary, Rashid Rauf, who organized the training of their respective leaders.[25] The London bombings murdered 52 people and injured hundreds more on July 7, 2005.[26] Two weeks later, an attempt to duplicate them failed. Its leader had cut off contact with Rauf after his return to London and never learned about a defect in the manufacturing of the bombs, which caused them to fail.[27] In the third attack, Rauf kept in close communications with the conspirators, which eventually led to their discovery. Seven suicide bombers and two bomb makers were arrested in Britain, while Rauf was arrested in Pakistan.[28] This second wave was the second most intense campaign of violence launched by al Qaeda against the West.

The third al Qaeda wave consisted of seven plots involving 21 terrorists (three individuals per attack) and mostly targeted northern Europe. In the Glasvej plot, a Danish-born son of Pakistani immigrants who was raised and radicalized in Pakistan, where he joined al Qaeda, returned to Copenhagen, where he recruited his young roommate. They tested a bomb detonator before the Danish authorities arrested them.[29]

Linking the next three plots was "Ahmad," an individual in Peshawar, Pakistan, serving as a communication link with al Qaeda.[30] In Operation Pathway, several friends from northwest Pakistan came to Manchester to carry out a terrorist operation. British intelligence intercepted their communications but had to arrest them prematurely after an official inadvertently displayed their identities to the press.[31] In the second plot, an e-mail from Denver to "Ahmad" asking questions about bomb making alerted the FBI, which followed its sender to New York City in Operation Highrise and identified his two accomplices. The leader had traveled back and forth to visit family in Peshawar, where he was radicalized because of the surge in drone attacks against Pashtuns. The three plotters were arrested before they could carry out simultaneous bombings in the New York City subway.[32] In the Oslo plot, an immigrant to Norway trained by al Qaeda recruited two fellow immigrants to carry out a bombing attack. The police, who had been monitoring the leader's communication with "Ahmad," arrested the conspirators after they bought chemicals that could be used to build a bomb.[33] Apparently "Ahmad" was not as hands-on in his handling of the three plot leaders as Rauf had been in the second wave, implying a lesser degree of al Qaeda control.

The shift to northern Europe in the third wave was partially due to the *Jyllands Posten*'s publication of insulting cartoons of the Prophet, which generated widespread protests and demonstrations in the Muslim world. The Danes and their prime minister viewed their publication as reflecting Western freedom of expression, but the Muslim world viewed them as an intentional provocation, an insult to the Prophet and to themselves as Muslims. The Mickey Mouse Project was an attempt by the person who had done the casing for the devastating Lashkar e-Toiba (LeT) Mumbai attacks at the end of 2008 to kill the cultural editor of the Danish newspaper. After LeT told its operative to stand down after the Mumbai attacks, he went to an al Qaeda leader, who approved his plan. He had traveled twice to Copenhagen to case his target and was on his way back there to execute it when he was arrested.[34]

In another incident related to the cartoons, four Tunisian immigrants to Sweden, some of whom had trained with al Qaeda, tried to carry out an attack on *Jyllands Posten*, which turned into a farce. They drove to Copenhagen and, on their way, their two leaders got into a fight: one of them was abandoned at the side of the highway and forced to hitchhike back home. The others arrived in Copenhagen in the middle of the night, and they got lost for hours. They had been detected by Swedish intelligence, and waiting Danish police finally ended their ordeal by arresting them. A police expert testified that he had never seen such incompetence in his 25 years of service: their assault rifle was "junk. . . . The bullets jammed, the magazine fell out and . . . it was nearly impossible to get it to fire more than one round at a time."[35] A Danish court found all of them guilty of terrorism.[36]

The final al Qaeda plot was the Düsseldorf plot. The leader of the plot recruited three university friends after his return from Pakistan, where al Qaeda had trained him. They were arrested while making explosives.[37] This third wave was not as serious a threat as the first two: all its plots/attacks failed to achieve their goals.

As the preceding discussion makes clear, the geographical targets of al Qaeda changed over time. All four incidents within the first four months after 9/11 targeted the United States, either at home or abroad. Six of the next seven plots targeted British civilians at home. Most of the last plots targeted Northern Europe. Specific opportunities for al Qaeda to launch attacks probably dictated these shifts. At first, it took advantage of the relative ease of travel for Saudi tourists to come to the United States and for European Muslims to return home from Afghanistan. When the United States made such travel more difficult, al Qaeda turned to Britain and its Pakistani Muslim population, which regularly visits relatives in Pakistan. Finally, when British people of Pakistani descent came under more intense scrutiny, al Qaeda made use of Muslim immigrants to northern Europe.

Of the 87 individuals involved in all its attacks, al Qaeda infiltrated 22 to the West specifically for the purpose of carrying out operations there—17 in the 9/11 attacks,[38] one in the Glasvej Plot, and four in Pathway. All the others, almost three-fourths of the total, had been radicalized in the West and then went to Pakistan or were recruited in the West by friends who had gone there. So the vast majority of al Qaeda linked jihadis did not infiltrate the West from the outside but were already in the West, and most did not travel abroad at all.

Al Qaeda Affiliates' Plots/Attacks in the West

Al Qaeda was not the only global neojihadi organization launching attacks on the West. Eight incidents were linked to other terrorist organizations, occurring at a steady rate of about one per year. The first one, the *al Tawhid wa'l Hijra* Plot (incident 8), involved Jordanian refugees in Germany, who planned a series of bombings against Jewish targets and nightclubs but were arrested before they could carry them out. In another, Lashkar e-Toiba trained a Pakistani Australian and a French Caribbean convert and directed them to carry out bombings in Sydney (incident 13). A collaborative Franco-Australian effort disrupted the plot in October 2003.[39] And in late 2004, immigrant sympathizers of *Ansar al Islam* in Germany tried to assassinate Iraqi Prime Minister Allawi during a state visit, but the German police arrested them before they could carry out the plot (incident 22).

The Sauerland Plot (incident 39) was the most serious plot to target Germany. Four friends, two German converts to Islam and two Turkish-Germans, wanted to fight in Chechnya or Iraq but were diverted by a facilitator in Turkey to the Islamic Jihad Union in Waziristan, where they were turned around after extensive training. They returned to Germany, collected large amounts of concentrated hydrogen peroxide, bought three trucks, and smuggled a dozen industrial detonators through Turkey. When they started boiling down the chemical to concentrate it to explosive strength, German authorities moved in and arrested them.[40]

Waziristan was where another terrorist group emerged when Pashtun elements opposed to the Pakistani government consolidated into an umbrella organization, the Tarik e-Taliban e-Pakistan. It launched a campaign of bombings in Pakistan, one of which killed former Pakistani Prime Minister Benazir Bhutto. In addition to its activities in Pakistan, it also projected its power into the West, plotting an attack on the Barcelona metro (incident 40). Of 12 people of Pakistani and Indian origin arrested, seven were legal residents of Spain while the others had allegedly been ordered to Barcelona to become suicide bombers. The police discovered only small amounts of explosives and just five of those charged were convicted—and only of belonging to a terrorist organization rather than conspiracy.[41] In other activity carried out in the West, the TTP trained a naturalized US citizen, who had come to the United States to study in the late 1990s, settled down, and married but then became radicalized and returned to Peshawar to live in a Muslim country. There, outraged by the drone campaign that was killing fellow Pashtuns, he contacted the TTP to help him retaliate against the United States. The TTP trained him and funded his plan to carry out a campaign of bombings in the United States. He returned to the United States, where he rigged a sport utility vehicle into a bomb and parked it in Times Square. The bomb caught fire but did not detonate (incident 55). He was arrested two days later trying to leave the country.[42]

At the end of the decade, al Qaeda in the Arabian Peninsula (AQAP) in Yemen became the most aggressive global neojihadi terrorist group targeting the West. While the vast majority of its operations were local, it did conduct two sophisticated attacks on the West. The first occurred on Christmas Day 2009, when a young Nigerian, who had become radicalized in London and then volunteered his services to AQAP's ideologue, Anwar al Awlaki, tried to detonate a bomb hidden in his underwear on a trans-Atlantic flight above Detroit (incident 53). Alert passengers and staff subdued him, and he was arrested on landing. In the second incident, AQAP hid bombs in printers on two separate cargo planes and set them to explode over US airspace (incident 59). Collaborating intelligence services intercepted the bombs before they could reach US airspace.

Mercifully, none of the al Qaeda–affiliated plots were successful. Al Qaeda affiliates sent nine people (five in the *al Tawhid* Plot and four in the Barcelona Plot) to infiltrate the West specifically for terrorist operations. All the other perpetrators had been radicalized in the West; some had gone to Pakistan or Yemen to become terrorists. Thus global neojihadi organizations, al Qaeda and its affiliates combined, launched 24 attacks against the West in the post-9/11 decade but succeeded in causing damage in only two of them (incidents 1 and 25), while four more were near misses (incidents 5, 26, 53, and 55). These organizations sent only 31 terrorists to infiltrate the West and carry out attacks there.

Chapter 1

Homegrown Global Neojihadi Plots in the West

The survey shows that the majority of the global neojihadi plots or attacks in the West came from homegrown
groups or individuals who had no significant connection
to any foreign terrorist organization. They constitute 42
plots/attacks (64 percent of the total) and involve 102 individuals (46 percent of the total), averaging 2.5 conspirators per incident.

So homegrown incidents dominate the overall shape
of the timeline frequency graphs. Figure 5 breaks those
attacks into incidents by groups and by loners, who did not
share their plans with their peers but were still part of the
global neojihadi community, often through virtual communication. The loner incidents represented almost half of
the homegrown plots/attacks (20 out of 42, or 48 percent)
and became more common at the end of the decade—

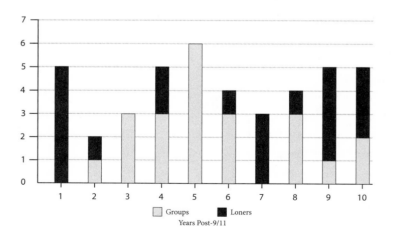

Figure 5. Homegrown Plots/Attacks in the Ten Years Post-9/11

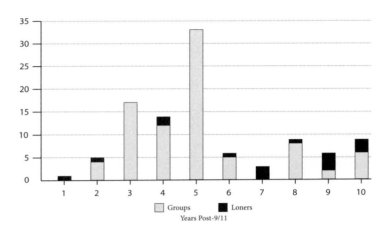

Figure 6. Homegrown Neojihadis in the Ten Years Post-9/11

70 percent in the last two years. Some loner attacks, though, were carried out by the same individual, for example Domenico Quaranta in Italy, who conducted four attacks before he was detected and arrested.[43] More fruitful for trend analysis, however, than the number of incidents is the distribution of homegrown global neojihadis. Figure 6 shows their distribution over time.

From figures 5 and 6, it is clear that there was a peak in homegrown incidents in the second quarter of the decade, which corresponds to the two and a half years after the 2003 invasion of Iraq. More than 60 percent of the total number of homegrown individuals were active during the period of this peak. This finding is consistent with the argument that one of the main stimuli of global neojihadi violence in the West was the Western invasion of Iraq. Militant Muslims felt outraged at this unjustified invasion of a Muslim land—a war on Islam in their worldview. This was compounded by Western official lies about the link between Saddam Hussein and the 9/11 attacks and the existence of weapons of mass destruction in Iraq.[44] Muslim militants spontaneously rebelled against their own Western countries and carried out attacks on behalf of victimized Muslims in Iraq and Afghanistan.

Although many homegrown plots/attacks were one-man (or -woman) shows, some of them involved large groups of people. At least 14 people were directly involved in the violence of the Madrid bombings (incident 14), about 12 were involved in the Dutch Hofstad/Piranha group (incidents 17, 21, 23, and 27),[45] and another 14 were involved in the Australian Pendennis Plot, evenly divided between Melbourne and Sydney groups (incident 29).[46] As I show later, bunches of violent guys (or terrorists) emerge out of domestic political protest communities to initiate and carry out their plots/attacks on their own, without notifying their friends from their networks. This progression leads to confusion, because some commentators assume that domestic terrorists must be completely isolated from these loose networks in order to be categorized as homegrown. But in our interconnected world today, assuming that homegrown terrorist groups are completely unconnected to other domestic or international political groups is unrealistic.

For instance, a few of the Madrid bombers were closely linked to a militant network that had been eliminated two years before they started plotting their attack in the fall of 2003. They were no longer in contact with their former friends, who were in prison or had fled the country. One scholar has repeatedly claimed for the past decade that there was a link between al Qaeda and the Madrid bombers, but fails to provide any evidence for it from the discovery material or the transcripts of the Madrid bombers' trial.[47] After much extensive search for this link within the intelligence community and in the field, including Madrid, Tetuan, and Tangiers, I have failed to discover this evidence.[48]

Just like the Madrid conspirators, the participants in the various Hofstad/Piranha incidents knew each other from childhood and emerged out of a larger Dutch/Moroccan Salafi community in the Netherlands. And in Australia, the 2009 Holsworthy Barracks plotters in Sydney (Operation Neath, incident 48)[49] were loosely connected with *al Shabaab* supporters in Australia and peripherally linked to some of the convicted participants of incident 29, who, in turn, were also loosely connected with a conspirator of incident 13. All these different Australian groups belonged to a loose political protest community. However, there was no evidence that any of the conspirators confided in or took direction from these other militant networks, domestic or foreign. Indeed, when the Operation Neath plotters tried to get the sanction of an *al Shabaab* preacher in Somalia for their plot, he refused. This did not stop them from proceeding with their plot.

Confusion exists as well in regard to loners' links to other extremists. Some label terrorists as lone wolves if they carry out an attack by themselves, as did Richard Reid, the shoe bomber, despite the fact that he was trained and directed by al Qaeda.[50] This is simply inaccurate: an organization's operative on a solo mission, such as a lone assassin or a sniper, is not a lone wolf. Others assume that for someone to be a lone wolf, he or she must be completely isolated as well from any political community. This does not make sense: violent political actors must be —

part of a political community in order to be "political." To me, a loner is a participant in a larger political community, either physically or virtually, who acts alone, without direction from any other person. Most loners were linked to such a community but acted alone, like Mohammed Bouyeri, a member of the Hofstad group, who killed Dutch filmmaker Theo van Gogh on his own, much to the surprise of his acquaintances (incident 21). He was a loner—he acted alone—but was not a "lone wolf" because he was an integral member of a close-knit community of militants.[51] Completely independent loners, such as Roshonara Choudhry, who stabbed British Member of Parliament Stephen Timms (incident 56), are rare, but even she participated in global neojihadi forums online.

The increasing presence of loners in attacks has an important implication. As the data in the survey shows, compared to those linked to foreign terrorist organizations, homegrown global neojihadi incidents had fewer conspirators involved in them—an average of about 2.5 versus about 4.8. Indeed, 20 homegrown incidents were carried out by 17 loners (as mentioned earlier, Quaranta carried out four of them). This low number made them far more difficult to detect than groups directed from abroad. As the previous sections noted, of 24 foreign terrorist organization-linked incidents, six (25 percent) went undetected, and only two (8 percent) were successful in causing any injury. For homegrown incidents, 19 went undetected (45 percent), and seven were successful in causing any serious injuries to innocent victims (17 percent).[52] Most of the undetected plots failed, because the bombs did not explode, they caused only minor injuries, or they injured or killed only the bomber. Although the successful homegrown attacks killed far fewer people than the two successful al Qaeda attacks, one of them, the Madrid bombings, killed 191 people and wounded about 1,500 more. Perhaps a reason behind the success of the Madrid bombers was the fact that they did not have to make their bombs from scratch, as they obtained industrial dynamite and detonators and only had to assemble their devices into effective bombs. With this exception, all the homegrown neojihadis who tried to manufacture bombs failed. The six other successful homegrown attacks used firearms (incidents 21, 46, 52, and 63) or knives (incidents 12 and 56). For homegrown terrorists, the simpler the plot, the more likely it is to succeed.

The Evolution of the Global Neojihadi Terrorist Threat

These timeline graphs help assess the two main views about the evolution of the global neojihadi threat in the West. There has been a famous controversy on two issues regarding this threat: its nature and structure—whether it was leader-led or leaderless—and whether al Qaeda was on the run or on the move at the end of the decade. I discussed the leaderless jihad in the introduction, where I pointed out that the global neojihadi threat was shifting from al Qaeda itself to a more homegrown one—al Qaeda on the run. In response, my critics have called homegrown terrorism a myth, arguing that, on the contrary, the threat from al Qaeda was increasing—al Qaeda on the move.[53]

The data here shows just 31 out of 220 global neojihadis infiltrated the West; we would expect such infiltration in top-down operations. Only 14 percent came from abroad, while 86 percent were radicalized at home and a few went abroad for training before returning home to sow death and destruction in the West. If we take out the 9/11 attacks, which were an outlier in the sample, we are left with only 12 infiltrators out of a total of 197, or just six percent of the total. This data strongly supports my 2008 analysis that the global neojihadi threat to the West emerged overwhelmingly from the bottom up, a homegrown movement of people self-radicalized, with a few volunteering to go abroad for training with a foreign terrorist organization and returning home to carry out attacks.

Recently, an edited book resurrected this controversy by arguing that the global neojihadi threat to the West was still mostly leader-led.[54] While its authors promised to "focus on most of the post-9/11 jihadist attacks and foiled attempts that occurred in Western countries since 2002,"[55] they only presented 13 case studies, two of which never even existed.[56] So they looked at only 11 incidents[57] out of a possible 60 (instead of 66 because they did not include the 9/11 attack, collapsed the four Dutch cases into one, and closed their list in May 2011 instead of going to September 2011). Their small sample was not representative of the whole set of incidents: al Qaeda and other terrorist organization incidents were overrepresented (8 out of 11, or 73 percent), while my comprehensive survey showed that these cases made up only 40 percent of the total. Their sample is bunched from March 2004 to January 2008, completely neglecting the last quarter of the post-9/11 decade, which makes it difficult to make any statement about any trend at the end of the decade. By stacking al Qaeda cases in their sample and selectively looking at the second quarter of the decade, at the height of the intensity of al Qaeda's campaign of violence in the West, they drew erroneous conclusions from their biased sample and ignored standard social science methodology.

In contrast, my *complete survey* of the global neoji-hadi threat in the West in the post-9/11 decade shows that it was overwhelmingly homegrown (leaderless), that it developed mostly from the bottom up, and that al Qaeda was indeed on the run in the second half of the decade. In fact, neither the top-down nor bottom-up perspective is accurate. They both emerge from a common process of the turn to political violence, which is elaborated in chapter 4. What the survey has shown is that there was a shift from top-down to bottom-up operations in the course of the post-9/11 decade. Before examining this process, the next chapter will first address the implications of the scope of this threat, which my survey helps to quantify. From the total number of global neojihadi involved in the threat against the West, we can derive the global neojihadi base rate (number of such terrorists per given population per year). This base rate gives us the magnitude of the probability of anyone becoming a terrorist, a critical value that should inform rational policy to deal with this threat.

Before moving on, a quick word on the current global neojihadi threat to the West, namely the one from Daesh. This threat is relatively new and emerged in the spring of 2014 when Daesh managed to capture a large territory in Northern and Western Iraq due to the collapse of the Iraqi Army. I have not included these new cases in my survey because their investigations are still in progress. Over the past year, there has been a great deal of hysteria about Daesh in the United States despite the fact that not a single Daesh oper-ative has yet been discovered in the country. Politicians fuel this panic, like they did for al Qaeda, and their exaggerated claims are faithfully transmitted by uncritical journalists, just like they were in the run-up to the 2003 invasion of Iraq. Some homegrown terrorists have carried out operations in the United States, most prominently in Garland, Texas, San Bernardino, California, and Orlando, Florida, but no link has yet been found to Daesh. Minutes before their respective attacks, the perpetrators sent messages claiming allegiance to Daesh. As such they resemble the homegrown terrorists described in this chapter, who carried out their operations in the West as retaliation for victims of Western killings in the Middle East. Daesh attacks in Europe are quite different from those in the United States because French-speaking terrorists had literally driven back and forth to the battle-fields in Syria and Iraq, where they were trained. There was a strong physical connection between Daesh and them. Daesh is a clear threat in the Middle East, where it has established itself as a real state. Its various attacks in Iraq and Syria are no longer terrorism but true war operations in two respec-tive civil wars. Attacks on civilians are unfortunately quite common in modern wars, despite the clear ban in interna-tional treaties. Western countries' involvement in these inter-nal wars makes them enemies in the eyes of Daesh and its Western sympathizers and therefore legitimate targets. So far, all the attacks in the United States on behalf of Daesh were carried out by these sympathizers and not refugees from Syria or Iraq. Closing US borders to refugees would not affect this threat, but bombing Daesh in the Middle East would. In contradiction to the Bush administration's argu-ment, fighting them there means we should expect to fight them here as well.

C h a p t e r 2

Probability Theory and Counterterrorism

In dealing with any social issue, its nature and scope should guide policy recommendations. Traditionally, political protesters wanted to advertise their cause to the public in what was called "propaganda by the deed," or as Brian Jenkins put it, "Terrorists want a lot of people watching, not a lot of people dead."[1] But over the past few decades, indiscriminate massacres like the Oklahoma City bombings and 9/11 attacks show that publicity no longer satisfies terrorists, who want to inflict the maximum number of casualties in retaliation and punishment for state deeds, at home or abroad. Faced with this escalation of the threat, states began to revise their practices. They moved away from usual criminal justice practices punishing captured perpetrators after their crimes toward ones preventing potential terrorists from committing their acts in the first place.

This shift in strategy takes different forms in different states, according to their traditions in dealing with political crimes.[2] Over the past two centuries, Western liberal democracies have evolved to guarantee for their citizens freedom from arbitrary confinement, freedom of speech, freedom of association, freedom of travel, and freedom from unreasonable searches. However, the new trend in political violence has halted this march to liberalism, and Western states have partially rolled back some of these freedoms. In Britain, freedom of expression has been limited to prevent the "glorification of terrorism." In France, laws against "participation in an association of malefactors whose goals is to prepare a terrorist act" erode freedom of association. In the United States, where freedom of speech and association are enshrined in the First Amendment of the Constitution, the government prosecutes suspected terrorists using laws against vaguely defined crimes such as conspiracies and material support for terrorism. The scope of these laws has been dramatically expanded over the past two decades and allows entrapment of naïve Muslim militants into committing crimes that would never have occurred absent FBI inducement. As a result, most Western liberal democracies have watered down individual civil rights and locked up people they label terrorists in what amounts to preventive detention.

Reverend Bayes Meets Counterterrorism

The identification of a potential terrorist is an exercise in probability since the potential perpetrator has not (yet) actually broken the law. How do we estimate the probability of someone carrying out a terrorist act? The probability of an individual about whom we know nothing carrying out such an act is what is called the "base rate" of terrorism. When we add more knowledge about the suspected individual (called a condition in probability theory), we can gauge more precisely the probability that he or she will engage in a violent terrorist act in the near future. This probability increases or decreases from the base rate according to the new information. Any attempt to detect and identify a terrorist relies on this conditional probability, made famous by the eighteenth-century English mathematician Reverend Thomas Bayes.

The first step in calculating this probability is to determine the actual base rate of terrorists in a given population. The survey in the previous chapter listed 66 global neojihadi serious plots or attacks, comprising 220 individuals, directly involving violence in the West in the post-9/11 decade. This amounts to an average of about six and a half serious incidents involving 22 individuals per year. Given a population of about 700 million people in the West,[3] this comes to about three new terrorists per 100 million Westerners per year. However, the perpetrators of this wave of political violence are Muslims and this fact (a new condition for computing this probability) dramatically increases the base rate among Muslims. The Muslim population in the West is unknown, but most estimates put it around 25 million. Thus 22 perpetrators in a population of about 25 million gives a base rate of new terrorists of a bit less than one per million Muslims in the West per year. So the condition of being Muslim increases the probability of being a terrorist 33-fold over the base rate in the general population. On the other hand, this very low probability means that more than 999,999 out of a million Muslims are not terrorists and should not be arrested on suspicion of terrorism.

This low base rate belies the contention of political spin-maestros and an uncritical press that 220 terrorists, armed with knives, guns, and homemade bombs (which didn't work most of the time) are as much of an existential threat as Nazi Germany and Japan during World War II or the Soviet Union during the Cold War. Only global amnesia, neglect of facts, and inability to make comparisons can support such baseless claims. The USSR, a country of 300 million people with thousands of nuclear weapons pointed at the United States and a military of several million people armed with very sophisticated weapons, could have completely destroyed the United States with its nuclear arsenal. The global neojihad poses a threat to the United States and the West, but it does not rise to a level where it threatens their existence. To put this threat in context, car accidents and US firearm homicides pose threats to Western and US lives several orders of magnitude higher than does the global neojihad.

The above numbers, which give an approximate estimate of this threat in the West, should guide our reactions and policies rather than the very improbable "worst-case scenarios" commonly used by Western politicians and counterterrorism officials. It is of course necessary to analyze worst-case scenarios and try to prevent them, but policies that deprive an individual of fundamental rights must be based on more than panic. They must be based on a realistic threat or probability that this individual might carry out serious acts of violence. The government's failure of imagination may have contributed to the tragedy of 9/11, but it has overreacted and its fanciful imagination now sees threats where they don't exist. Politicians' fearmongering may come from a genuine misunderstanding of the level of the threat, or it may simply represent a cynical attempt to advance their political careers.

Instead of educating the public about the real magnitude of the threat, many politicians encourage their constituents' worst fears and fuel them to the point of hysteria. This "needless alarm, exaggerated portrayals of the terrorist threat, unrealistic expectations of a risk-free society, and unreasonable demands for absolute protection will only . . . make America fibrillate in fear and bankrupt itself with security."[4]

Alarmists succeed because the judgment necessary to gauge the dangerousness of an individual, a problem in conditional probability, is subject to common biases and flawed thinking. Daniel Kahneman and Amos Tversky discovered that people usually commit common errors in judgments when confronted with specific Bayesian problems because the correct answer often seems counterintuitive.[5] They demonstrated these errors by asking people apparently simple problems:

> A cab was involved in a hit and run accident at night. Two cab companies, the Green and the Blue, operate in the city . . . 85 percent of the cabs in the city are Green and 15 percent are Blue. A witness identified the cab as Blue. The court tested the reliability of the witness under the same circumstances that existed on the night of the accident and concluded that the witness correctly identified each one of the two colors 80 percent of the time and failed 20 percent of the time. What is the probability that the cab involved in the accident was Blue rather than Green?

Most college graduates answered 80 percent, which was the tested accuracy of the witness.[6] However, the correct answer is only 41 percent, as determined by a simple calculation using Bayes' Theorem. This seems counterintuitive to our common way of thinking, which often disregards the base rate of a phenomenon as irrelevant—a reasoning flaw called base rate neglect. This is just one example of the typical judgmental errors made by people, which Kahneman and Tversky call "heuristics [cognitive shortcuts] and biases."

More than a Hunch: Sensitivity and Specificity

The usefulness of a behavioral indicator, or a probability condition, in predicting the potential of someone to commit a violent terrorist act is based on its *sensitivity* and *specificity*. An example of sensitivity in daily life occurs in the practice of medicine. Physicians commonly use indicators, or laboratory tests, in making diagnoses. Sensitivity of a medical test measures the proportion of correctly identified positives (in medicine, the percentage of sick people who are correctly identified as having the disease). This proportion is the ratio of the number of true positives (correctly diagnosed sick people) over the total number of positives—the sum of true positives plus false negatives (the total number of sick people, which is the number of people correctly identified as sick plus those incorrectly identified as healthy). Thus, in terrorism, the sensitivity of an indicator would be the ratio of correctly identified terrorists over the total number of true terrorists.

Specificity of an indicator measures the proportion of correctly identified negatives (in the medical example, the percentage of correctly identified healthy people). It is

the ratio of the number of true negatives (correctly identified healthy people) over the number of true negatives
plus the number of false positives (or the total number of
healthy individuals: the number of people correctly identified as healthy plus those healthy people misdiagnosed
as sick). In assessing terrorism, the specificity of an indicator is the ratio of nonterrorists identified as such over
the total number of nonterrorists. The evaluation of the
specificity of an indicator of terrorism requires the meaningful comparison of nonterrorists to terrorists in relation
to that indicator. To my knowledge, except for my own
classified work, no government has ever tested the validity of any of its indicators. In other words, no government
knows the rate of error resulting from using indicators to
identify a suspected terrorist.

Sensitivity and specificity are related in a complex
way, and there is usually a trade-off between these measures to calibrate an appropriate "signal-to-noise" ratio
for the identification of a given case. In terrorism, given
the potential gravity of a single attack, we should lean
to identify all potential terrorists—in scientific terms, to
maximize sensitivity over specificity. For instance, at air-
port security, scanners are usually set to trigger on low-
risk items like belt buckles and keys (low specificity) in
order to catch all metallic threats such as firearms or
bombs (high sensitivity). So let's assume that a government has developed an instrument or profile to identify
potential terrorists based on "derogatory information"
about individuals that has 100 percent sensitivity but only
near perfect specificity, say 99 percent. This type of near-
perfect accuracy has rarely been achieved in the physical
sciences and is unheard of in the social sciences. Under

our hypothetical assumptions, this instrument is 100 percent sensitive and therefore would catch all the potential terrorists. However, in terms of specificity, this instrument would make one error in one hundred evaluations (99 percent specificity) and erroneously identify an innocent person as a terrorist in one hundred assessments.

The rate of error—that is, the proportion of people incorrectly identified—of the instrument depends on the base rate of terrorists in the population. To demonstrate this, let's assume a population of about a million people, 100 of whom are terrorists. The instrument would identify all 100 terrorists for 100 percent sensitivity. However, it would make one error in each one hundred evaluations (99 percent specificity) and falsely identify another 10,000 people as terrorists. Despite the fact that this instrument is near perfect, the probability that a person identified as a terrorist by this instrument is actually a terrorist is less than 1 percent (100 correctly identified terrorists divided by the total number identified as terrorists by this instrument [100 + 10,000 = 10,100], or 100 divided by 10,100, which is a little less than 1 percent)!

In calculating probability, the rate of error is inversely proportional to the base rate: the lower the base rate of terrorists in this case, the greater the rate of error. For instance, if there is only 1 terrorist in one million people—the base rate of global neojihadis in the total Muslim population in the West—what is the probability of correctly identifying a terrorist with this near-perfect instrument, test, or profile? The police would catch the lone terrorist (100 percent sensitivity), but would also make one error in one hundred assessments (99 percent specificity), which identifies a further 10,000 people as terrorists (1 percent of a million). Therefore, the probability of correctly identifying a terrorist with this near-perfect instrument is about 0.01 percent (1 divided by 10,001)! Put it another way, its rate of error is 99.99 percent (10,000 incorrectly identified divided by 10,001 identified by the instrument).

If all the various police departments in the West collaborate and carry out a gigantic sweep by applying this profile to their respective Muslim populations in order to catch terrorists hiding in their respective societies, they would arrest all 22 terrorists that emerge in a given year. However, they would make a mistake 1 percent of the time for 25 million people, which comes to 250,000 people. Therefore, in order to catch all new 22 global neo-jihadi terrorists, they would put 250,000 Muslims in jail by mistake. This rate of error of 99.99 percent is simply not acceptable in a liberal democracy. The reason that the instrument or profile is so misleading despite the fact that it is near perfect is because there are so many more nonterrorists than terrorists. Let me further illustrate this point with the most famous of the government watchlists.

Nomination to the No Fly or Selectee Lists

Low base rate neglect has real-life consequences. Some Muslims wrongly suspected of having a "predisposition" to carry out a terrorist act are set up by the FBI in sting operations and are later sentenced to very long prison terms (about 25 years). More Muslims are put on the US No Fly and Selectee Lists, which violates their freedom to travel. People are nominated to this list based not on scientific reasoning but on a flawed intuitive hunch.

Government watchlists have been uncritically accepted by the general public. In fact, recently there were discussions about banning people on these watchlists from buying a firearm. But how accurate are these government terrorist watchlists, including the No Fly and Selectee Lists? Who is included in them?

Over time, the No Fly List has evolved from a focus on direct threats to aviation to a less discriminating one lumping together all enemies of the United States and its allies. Prior to 9/11, the FBI administered a list of individuals that posed a "known threat to civil aviation." This was confined to "any person . . . who represents a threat of committing an act of international terrorism or domestic terrorism with respect to an aircraft."[7] On September 11, 2001, there were only 16 individuals identified as "no transport."[8] The 9/11 attacks demonstrated the previously unimaginable devastations that came from using airplanes as terrorist weapons, and within two months, the Transportation Security Administration (TSA) was created. It assumed responsibility for the list, which was split into "No Fly" and "Automatic Selectee" lists to "secure commercial air travel against the threat of terrorism. Individuals on the No Fly List are prohibited from boarding a U.S. commercial aircraft . . . Individuals on the Selectee List must undergo enhanced security screening."[9] The lists' purposes dramatically expanded to include "any person . . . who represents a threat of committing an act of 'domestic terrorism' with respect to the homeland."[10] Here, the list specifically designed to protect aviation no longer requires any threat linked to aviation. This second criterion for inclusion opened up the floodgates for nomination and, by the fall of 2002, the No Fly List was already plagued by the problem of false positives.[11] Nevertheless, the enlarged pool of suspects that resulted was still deemed to be too limiting because it did not include threats to US military bases overseas, and so it was expanded to any "threat of committing an act of international terrorism against any U.S. Government facility abroad and any associated or supporting personnel."[12] Any Taliban in Afghanistan lobbing a mortar at a US military facility to defend his country against foreign invasion is defined as a terrorist and therefore prohibited from boarding a plane.

Even this was not enough. A fourth criterion was adopted and included anyone detained at Guantanamo Bay unless certified as posing no threat by the US president. This new criterion added "flexibility" by dropping the requirement of targeting US interests. It now included "any threat of engaging in or conducting a violent act of terrorism" by anyone anywhere in the world who is "operationally capable," meaning having "the ability, knowledge, opportunity, and intent or . . . actively seeking the opportunity to engage in a violent act of terrorism." For example, "operational capability" may be indicated by someone "scouting potential targets or traveling for no legitimate purpose to places that have terrorist training grounds, regardless of whether the person is presently capable of using an IED."[13]

The requirement of violence for inclusion on the lists was also dropped in the definition of a *known terrorist*— "an individual . . . engaged . . . in terrorism and/or terrorist activities, including an individual who has been charged, arrested, indicted, or convicted for a crime *related* to terrorism by U.S. Government or foreign government authorities." For the purpose of inclusion on a watchlist, terrorism and terrorist activities are defined as "acts that involve violent acts or acts dangerous to human life, property, or infrastructure"[14] that violate US domestic law but are committed anywhere in the world and are political in nature. A footnote clarifies that violence is not required for terrorist acts—conscious acts of material support to anyone or any organization that has committed a terrorist activity or is planning to do so are also included. Such material support includes "providing a safe house, transportation, communications, funds, transfer of funds or any material benefit, false documentation or identification, weapons . . . or training for the commission of an act of terrorism and/or terrorist activity."[15] Since the overwhelming majority of people charged with a terrorist related crime face charges of material support for terrorism, this definition includes all those *nonviolent* offenders.

The category of "suspected terrorists" is even vaguer and includes individuals who *are acquitted or for whom charges are dismissed*; are identified as just belonging to a group engaging in terrorist activities, even *without any particularized derogatory information*; are identified as terrorists by a foreign government; are identified as associates of known or suspected terrorists; or are identified as fundraisers, document forgers, travel facilitators, money launderers, and arms merchants—if an individual is engaging in any support, he should be *presumed to do so knowingly*. It also includes individuals who advocate, incite, or solicit others to produce imminent lawless action and are likely to produce such action; are identified as *sympathizers and supporters* of a terrorist organization; are identified as foreign fighters; are involved with terrorist-associated weapons; are identified in information found during raids on terrorist targets; were targeted in US military or intelligence raids; and are lone wolves.[16]

Nomination to the No Fly or Selectee Lists requires a minimum of identifying information (name, address, date and place of birth) and a minimum of substantive derogatory information. The nomination procedure is different for foreigners and "U.S. persons"—presumed to be citizens whose freedom of speech and peaceful assembly are preserved by First Amendment rights.[17] They are also protected from errors through periodic reviews that might correct erroneous information.[18] For the rest of the chapter, I focus exclusively on US persons nominated to the two lists.

Nomination to the lists requires a reasonable suspicion that an individual is a known or suspected terrorist. Reasonable suspicion is "based on the totality of the circumstances, must rely upon articulable intelligence or information which, taken together with rational inferences from those facts, reasonably warrants a determination that an individual is known or suspected" to engage in terrorist acts. "There must be an objective factual basis . . . Mere guesses or hunches are not sufficient to constitute a reasonable suspicion that an individual is a known or suspected terrorist."[19]

In addition, "particularized derogatory information . . . demonstrates the nature of an individual's or group's association with terrorism and/or terrorist activities that is descriptive and specific to an event or activity."[20] The National Counterterrorism Center's (NCTC) *Watchlisting Guidance* manual provides four such behavioral indicators to support a reasonable suspicion determination:

attendance at a terrorist training camp, attendance at a
facility teaching a violent extremist ideology, frequent contacts with preachers of hate, and travel for no known legitimate purpose to an area of terrorist activities.[21] In another
section, the manual provides six examples of behavioral
indicators of being operationally capable (of engaging in
terrorism): training as a terrorist, expression of desire to
become a martyr, indication of intent to participate in planning or conducting an attack, planning an attack, contacts
with terrorist facilitator, and association with terrorists and
accumulation of weapons.[22] The manual does not give any
scientific rationale for these ten indicators or their sensitivity or specificity, either singly or in various combinations.

Despite its length, consisting mostly of legal ver-
biage that stresses compliance with legal standards, there
is remarkably little in the manual about the actual decision making process of inclusion on the watchlists, only
vague normative prescriptions like "the totality of the
information is evaluated based on the experience of the
reviewer, and the facts and rational inferences that may
be drawn from those facts, including past conduct, current actions, and credible intelligence concerning future
conduct."[23] Government officials claim that nomination
is done by specifically trained subject matter experts with
demonstrated proficiency, "based on analysis of available
intelligence and investigative information that the person meets the applicable criteria for inclusion."[24] However, they decline to provide further details on the process
because it is often based on sensitive information showing
that the suspect is a target of a counterterrorism investigation, which could reveal sensitive sources and methods. They warn that disclosure of this information might

harm national security.[25] However, they still refuse to provide this information when a person is already on the No Fly List, which discloses that this person is a target of an investigation. Furthermore, this information contained in internal FBI e-mails is also routinely revealed at trial when the government goes on to prosecute such targets.

The Government's Unjustified Assumptions

The government's nomination procedure to the No Fly and Selectee Lists rests on multiple assumptions and methodological shortcuts. First and foremost, the government's concept of a terrorist is static and permanent according to past, present, or potential future action. To me, a terrorist is simply someone who carries an act of terrorism at a given time. Although there is no consensus about a definition of terrorism among scholars, the vast majority agree that it involves an act of violence (not just nonviolent support).[26] A politically violent person may later become nonviolent and indeed a champion of nonviolence. Our own rebellious founding fathers, who were surely terrorists to King George III, had the word existed then, tried to govern in peace. Resistance fighters against Nazis during World War II generated the peaceful leadership of postwar Europe and freedom fighters against colonial powers became peaceful leaders in the Third World. People labeled as violent terrorists at one time such as Le Duc Tho, Menachem Begin, Nelson Mandela, and Yasser Arafat went on to earn the Nobel Peace Prize. The point here is that people respond to their circumstances and act according to them, producing violence at one time and peace at another. Attributing a permanent quality or label, like terrorist, to them is not supported by empirical evidence.

The watchlist definition of terrorist shows the danger of a slippery slope of quickly enlarging a category originally limited to people directly engaged in political violence to people providing any kind of support to political groups fighting abroad. The expansion floods the category with obviously nonviolent people, who present no threat to anyone, let alone air transportation. Giving shelter for one night or a little money to a childhood friend in need earns a nomination to the lists if that friend is later suspected of being a terrorist. Having an erroneous terrorism-related charge dismissed is rewarded by assignment to the list. Asking advice on the Internet about one's failing marriage from a popular imam, suspected of being a terrorist, lands one on such a list. Simply hanging out with friends who are suspected terrorists may lead to inclusion on it. All these examples come from people I have interviewed or investigated.

The inclusion of "foreign fighters" is also troubling. Throughout history, people have traveled to foreign places to fight in the name of freedom. These include the Marquis de La Fayette, Tadeusz Kosciuszko, and Baron von Steuben in the American War of Independence; Lord Byron in the Greek War of Independence; George Orwell in the Spanish Civil War; American volunteers to fight the Nazis before the United States declared war on them; or Jews fighting for the nascent state of Israel. Now they would be included on a list as suspected terrorists. These people were not "suspected terrorists" but heroes precisely for engaging in violence against tyrants. The inclusion of foreign fighters is a blow to the liberation of oppressed people throughout the world.

There is a consensus among scholars that becoming a terrorist at a given time is a process and that most people could turn politically violent if put in a conducive situation. That process is similar to becoming a soldier. Recruits become soldiers over time and engage in violent combat regardless of their predisposition to violence. In my interviews with them, terrorists believed that they were soldiers defending their endangered community. Like soldiers, their potential to become politically violent is contextual and not dependent on personal predisposition (or personal indicators of violence). There is a window of circumstances and opportunities during which someone will engage in acts of terrorism and a much longer period when he or she will not. The desire to commit terrorist acts is dependent on a fluid mixture of personal and environmental factors, which changes all the time. Lists of "terrorists" or "suspected terrorists" do not monitor these changing factors but only check for accuracy of derogatory information at a specific time.

Once a label is put on someone and accepted by others, it acquires a power of its own and frames the way people think about that person. Removing that label requires great cognitive effort because it has become the default way of viewing that person. We are naturally biased animals and reluctantly change opinions; new information contradicting our default perspective must meet a much higher threshold than evidence that confirms that perspective. This is reflected in the difficulty in removing a suspect put on the No Fly or Selectee Lists from erroneous information. In my half dozen years monitoring the daily traffic of threats, I have noted that derogatory information usually flooded the threat matrix, while retractions or corrections were extremely rare in comparison. Indeed, the intelligence system encourages reporting derogatory information on US persons but discourages reporting disconfirming evidence.[27] Agents are promoted for providing derogatory information on US persons, but admission of error or finding new information exonerating someone from suspicion is not rewarded and may even have negative repercussions on their careers. The incentive is thus to report suspicious activity but not to correct false alarms. My experience in investigating terrorist suspects in the United States is that the FBI is very reluctant to close a case. In effect, it has low standards to open investigations but very high standards to close them or recommend deletion from a watchlist. The result is that most of the cases on these lists are probably legacies of past false alarms, which, combined with the presumption of static predisposition to violence, are seldom corrected, leading to a very high error rate.

Numbers for addition or deletion from the No Fly or Selectee Lists are classified and not available, but I was able to find information showing that from 2010 to 2013, the government added 430,000 people to the Terrorist Identities Datamart Environment (TIDE) but deleted only 50,000.[28] It is hard to believe that in three years the population of suspected terrorists worldwide grew by almost half a million while only 50,000 left terrorism. Although these numbers mostly deal with non-US persons, it illustrates how much easier it is to add a subject to a watchlist than to remove him or her from it, a ratio of about 9:1. I strongly suspect that the same is true for the No Fly and

Selectee Lists: it is relatively easy to put people on these lists and very difficult to take them off.

Biases and False Assumptions in the Watchlist Nomination Process

Developments in the cognitive sciences show that the types of judgments made in the watchlist nomination process are the product of common biases and flawed thinking. What the government believes is an unproblematic assessment is instead a complex exercise in Bayesian problem solving: given a specific piece of derogatory information, what is the probability that a subject will engage in a violent act of terrorism? Or more precisely, how does the condition of the new information change the base rate of terrorism to estimate the probability that this given individual will engage in a violent act of terrorism? Past a certain threshold of probability, that person should be considered a suspected terrorist and the degree of scrutiny (increased intrusive monitoring and resource allocation) should be proportional to the index of suspicion he or she generates. The result of this conditional prediction depends on the base rate of engaging in political violence. I am unaware that anyone within the government involved in the nomination process has carried out a Bayesian analysis of the derogatory information provided.

What is the base rate of a US person becoming a violent global neojihadi from the general US population? In the post-9/11 decade, table 1 identifies 17 US persons involved in nine global neojihadi incidents in the post-9/11 decade. To that number, I add Adnan al-Shukrijuma, peripherally involved in Pakistan in the NYC Subway Plot, for a total of 18. The very low number of US global neojihadis may be surprising in light of the Department of Justice's National Security Division's statement that there had been 494 convictions for terrorism related charges as of June 2012.[29] However, the vast majority of these charges were for nonviolent acts—material support, wanting to go abroad and fight there as a "foreign fighter," or being caught in sting operations from which, as the government assured the public, there was never any danger. In all these sting operations, the FBI provided the means to carry out an attack, and the entrapped individuals lacked the ability to carry out any attack. The vast majority of arrests were therefore not for a threat of violence on the homeland.

The government argues that it foiled many other attacks that did not become public, but this is very unlikely in terrorism cases, where the government's appetite for publicity is insatiable. All the arrests, even for trivial crimes such as paying $500 to a friend suspected of having terrorist connections, have been widely publicized as "major victories" in the war on terror. The government may have a stronger argument in claiming that it prevented potential terrorists from traveling abroad to get some training and returning to attack the United States domestically or preventing US persons abroad from returning and causing mayhem at home. However, most "foreign fighters" want to fight abroad, not to come back and attack the homeland. A few do, as table 1 shows in several al Qaeda cases. In this country, out of hundreds of foreign fighters, Zazi, Ahmadzay, Medunjanin, and Shahzad are the only four who were turned around by a foreign terrorist organization and came back to attack the homeland.

Table 2 lists all the real US global neojihadis who threatened or carried out attacks in the West. The first column provides the incident number from table 1, and the second column the name of the US global neojihadi in question. The next ten columns are the ten behavioral indicators listed in the manual. To remind the reader, they were (1) attendance at a terrorist training camp (Camp), (2) attendance at a facility teaching a violent extremist ideology (Idea), (3) frequent contacts with preachers of hate (Preach), (4) travel for no known legitimate purpose to an area of terrorist activities (Trip), (5) training as a terrorist (Train), (6) expression of desire to become a martyr (Martyr), (7) indication of intent to participate in planning or conducting an attack (Intent), (8) planning an attack (Plan), (9) contacts with terrorist facilitator (Facil), and (10) association with terrorists and accumulation of weapons (Asstn). The signs (+) or (-) show the presence or absence of these indicators in each case.

US Global Neojihadis

The base rate of US global neojihadis is therefore 18 people over a period of ten years in a population of approximately 300 million people. This amounts to a rate of 0.6 US violent neojihadi per 100 million per year.[30] Usually such rates in the United States are standardized to per 100,000 people per year, which gives a rate of 0.0006 per 100,000 per year. To appreciate how low this base rate is, consider that in 2013, the US homicide rate was about

Table 2. US Persons in Global Neojihadi Post-9/11 Plots in the West

Incident	Name	Camp	Idea	Preach	Trip	Train	Martyr	Intent	Plan	Facil	Asstn
15	Mohammed Junaid Babar	+	-	-	+	-	-	+	-	-	+
24	Kevin James	-	-	-	-	-	-	+	-	-	-
24	Levar Washington	-	-	-	-	-	-	+	-	-	-
24	Gregory Patterson	-	-	-	-	-	-	+	-	-	-
24	Hammad Samana	-	-	-	-	-	-	+	-	-	-
46	Carlos Bledsoe	-	-	-	+	-	-	-	-	-	-
47	Daniel Boyd	+	-	-	+	+	-	+	-	-	+
47	Hysen Sherifi	-	-	-	-	-	-	+	-	-	+
49	Najibullah Zazi	+	-	-	-	+	+	+	+	+	+

Incident	Name	Camp	Idea	Preach	Trip	Train	Martyr	Intent	Plan	Facil	Asstn
49	Zarein Ahmadzay	+	-	-	-	+	+	+	+	-	-
49	Adis Medunjanin	+	-	-	+	+	+	+	+	-	-
49	Adnan al-Shukrijuma in the US	-	-	-	+	-	-	-	-	-	-
51	David Headley	+	-	+	-	+	-	+	+	+	+
52	Nidal Malik Hasan	-	-	+	-	-	-	-	+	-	-
53	Anwar al-Awalki in the US	-	-	-	-	-	-	-	-	-	-
55	Faisal Shahzad	+	-	-	-	+	-	+	+	-	+
59	Samir Khan in the US	-	-	-	+	-	-	-	-	-	-
66	Naser Abdo	-	-	-	-	-	-	+	+	-	+
	Sensitivity (%)	39	0	11	33	33	17	72	39	11	33

4.5 while the suicide rate was about 12.6 per 100,000 per year. In other words, the homicide rate is almost 7,000 times greater and the suicide rate is 20,000 times greater than the terrorist base rate in the United States. With such a low base rate, an instrument would have to be extremely accurate, especially in terms of specificity (greater than 99.99999 percent), for government agencies not to be drowned in false positives or false alarms. As I noted earlier, however, evaluating a base rate of global neojihadis in the total US population may not give a fair estimate since they are all Muslims. Considering only the US Muslim population, which most experts estimate to be about 1 percent of the total US population, gives 1.8 US global neojihadis per 3 million Muslims per year or 0.06 per 100,000 US Muslims per year. Any instrument trying to detect them would still have to be extremely accurate, with a specificity greater than 99.999 percent, to be of any value. But government analysts suffer from low base rate neglect in judging probability: they overestimate the probability of terrorists and underestimate the number of false positives. The *Watchlisting Guidance* compounds this problem by directing government officials to include people on the No Fly or Selectee Lists even though they present no violent threat to the US homeland.

The low number of US global neojihadis refutes a common argument justifying sting operations. Unlike prosecutors who argue to a jury that defendants in sting operations would have carried out terrorist operations because they are predisposed to do so (an empirically false assertion), FBI special agents close to the investigation know better. Their targets would never have conducted any operation had they been left on their own. FBI agents justify their sting operations by claiming, "We got to the suspects before al Qaeda did." This statement assumes that al Qaeda agents are present on US soil to meet with suspects. The data shows that, even from among the global neojihadis, there were only five individuals in the United States with any al Qaeda connections in this ten-year period (Babar, Zazi, Ahmadzay, Medunjanin, and Headley) and another with TTP connections. None of them was interested in recruiting new US persons and focused instead on accomplishing their respective operations. Al Qaeda or foreign terrorist organizations have such a small presence, let alone infrastructure, in the United States that they would never have "gotten" to the suspects.

Effectiveness of the No Fly and Selectee Lists in Protecting the United States

But aside from the ethics and politics of the No Fly and Selectee Lists, there is the question as well of their scientific validity. How effective are they in fulfilling their purpose—protection against global neojihadi threats?[31] I first examine the validity of each of the components of the two lists and then the lists as a whole.

In regard to how effective the ten behavioral indicators listed in the manual are at detecting potential US global neojihadis, to my knowledge, there has been no Bayesian analysis of their sensitivity or specificity. At one point, I was briefed on a large NCTC descriptive correlational analysis of various personal characteristics of all the US suspects, but those were mostly people charged and prosecuted for nonviolent terrorism related offenses like support. Instead, I focus only on the violent US global neojihadi listed in table 2 to analyze the sensitivity or specificity of the NCTC manual's ten indicators as applied to these individuals.

With the exception of intent to participate in planning or conducting an attack, none of the other indicators even reached the 50 percent sensitivity mark. Contrary to the conventional wisdom blaming ideology for this brand of terrorism, none attended a facility teaching a violent extremist ideology and only two had contact with ideologues, making ideological indicators poor predictors of the turn to violence. Attending training camps or getting terrorism training constitute almost the same action; they show a sensitivity of 39 percent and 33 percent, respectively.[32] Despite its low sensitivity, training at a terrorist camp is still a good indicator because it has a relatively high specificity—very few Western Muslims went to these camps. Likewise, travel (or attempt to travel) for no known legitimate purpose to an area of terrorist activity has a sensitivity of 33 percent but relatively high specificity. I would keep them both as indicators, but would caution that final determination to include someone in a watchlist would need to involve more assessment of the person's context at the time of the evaluation.

By far, the best indicators were, as noted, intent to participate in planning or conducting an attack (72 percent) and planning an attack (39 percent). Showing intent to participate in an attack has much less specificity than actually planning an attack because there is so much loose talk and braggadocio among young, militant Muslims, who want to appear tough in front of their peers. However, declaration of intent to participate in an attack is still worrisome and should be further investigated. The person should be increasingly monitored if more concrete preparation for such an attack is discovered, but not before that point, because the low specificity of this indicator would tie up too many resources. Note that indication of intent is not foolproof. The three US global neojihadis who went abroad (Shukrijuma, Awlaki, and Khan) did not show any indication of such intent before they left. They became involved in their respective attacks after a long time abroad. Two others did not indicate any intent.[33] I would keep both of these indicators with the same caution stated in the previous paragraph. The point this analysis makes clear is that all the indicators in the manual suffer from low sensitivity except for intent to plan or conduct an attack—but it lacked specificity. Overall, I found four of the ten indicators useful in detecting potential terrorists from a mixture of sensitivity and specificity.

As for the validity of the No Fly and Selectee Lists as a whole, the original No Fly List sought to protect civil aviation. None of the US global neojihadis in table 2 directly threatened to damage an aircraft. Two of them plotted together two attacks against air transport— Awlaki and Khan—but neither personally boarded a plane. Instead, in one attack, a Nigerian, Umar Farouk Abdulmutallab, carried an underwear bomb aboard an airplane (he was not put on the list despite the fact that his father had denounced him) and, in the other, they shipped unaccompanied printers with bombs in them. Putting Awlaki or Khan on the No Fly List would not have prevented these attacks. These two in Yemen and

Shukrijuma in Pakistan were probably the only three US global neojihadis put on a watchlist *before* they actually carried out attacks against the United States but *after* their departure from the United States. Probably several others were added to the lists, but *after* they were actually carrying out an attack, like Zazi, Ahmadzay, Medunjanin, or Shahzad. The lists would not have prevented them from carrying out their attacks. Therefore, only the three US global neojihadis abroad out of 18 were prevented from *personally* carrying out an attack in the United States, since being on the lists barred them from returning home for an attack in this country. This amounts to a 17 percent sensitivity (the correct identification of true terrorists) of the lists as instruments to prevent people from directly attacking civil aviation or the homeland. This poor result is an indictment of the effectiveness of the No Fly and Selectee Lists in protecting the United States against a US terrorist threat. I am not addressing its effectiveness against non-US persons, which I sincerely hope is better—but it is extremely difficult to assess without good data.

When we turn to the specificity of the watchlist assessment, the story is different. Recall that specificity is the correct identification of nonterrorists, thus preventing innocent people from losing their freedom to travel. To estimate the specificity of the watchlists, we need to know the number of US persons on the No Fly List. Although the government has not released this number, a leak showed that in August 2013, there were 47,000 people on the No Fly List, of whom 800 were US persons, and 16,000 people on the Selectee List, of whom 1,200 were US persons.[34] This means that the two lists identify

300 million minus 2,000 Americans as being nonterrorists, which gives an incredibly high specificity of 299,998,000 divided by 300,000,000 or 99.9993 percent! This came as a surprise to me, because I expected the government to sacrifice specificity for sensitivity in order to make sure it caught all potentially politically violent people. This very high specificity rate is indeed a credit to the government's restraint for putting people on the two lists despite its alarmist bias. This commendable restraint indicates that the government is indeed taking very seriously its duty to protect US persons' civil liberties.

As to who is on the No Fly and Selectee Lists from the United States, a quarter of them are the 500 or so charged, arrested, indicted, or convicted of terrorism related crimes mandated to be put on the lists. They are either incarcerated, closely watched, or deported and do not cause much of a threat to the United States at the time they are on the list. Given the terrorism enhancement to sentences, most convicted of terrorist offenses are incarcerated for a very long time and will not cause any problem in the near future. As I pointed out, the likelihood of turning politically violent is not permanent; in fact, it peaks between the ages of 18 and 30. So when these persons are released, they are not likely to turn to political violence but instead to attempt to move on with their lives. This is also my impression from my interviews of several of them in prison and after their release.

Three quarters of the people on the No Fly and Selectee Lists are terrorist suspects, using "terrorist" as it is defined in the manual.[35] The vast majority of them are nonviolent individuals who simply associated with suspected terrorists, "facilitated" some terrorist action (such as giving

shelter or money to friends), or even sympathized or supported a designated terrorist organization. For such nonviolent people, inclusion on the No Fly or Selectee Lists
is not protective of the United States but clearly punitive
without further due process.

To judge the rate of error for inclusion into the No
Fly and Selectee Lists, note that three US global neojihadis were correctly identified. There are probably more
true US global neojihadis on the lists—for instance, Ali
al Marri, Jose Padilla, Iyman Faris, and Christopher Paul
in the United States and Adam Gadahn, Majid Khan, and
Omar Hammami abroad—but they were not involved in
any plots or attacks against the homeland and were not
violent threats against the homeland. Correctly identifying three US violent global neojihadis out of 2,000 on the
list gives an error rate of 99.85 percent! The reason for this
enormous error rate is low base rate neglect in nominating people to the watchlists. Because the number of true
violent terrorists out of those fitting the criteria listed
in the manual is very small, about one hundred times
smaller than the total people on both lists, the rate of error
is very large. Even if I am wrong in my estimates and the
number of true terrorists is ten times greater, it would still
give an error rate of about 98 percent! So despite the great
effort of the government to preserve US personal civil liberties, its low base rate neglect and lack of understanding
of Bayesian probability still lead it to grossly overestimate
the violent terrorist threat and commit a very large number of assessment errors.

Even more disturbing, putting people on the watchlists may produce exactly the opposite of what these lists
are intended to accomplish. Inclusion in the lists may

actually accelerate the turn to violence, when there was previously a very low likelihood of such a turn, and create a terrorist where there was none, increasing the threat to the United States. The case of Mohamed Mohamud in Portland, Oregon, illustrates this self-fulfilling prophecy. During his senior year of high school, he hung around militant Islamists, and the government put him on the No Fly List despite the lack of any indication of violence at the time. He went away to college, where he partied, drank, smoked marijuana, and left Islam and militancy behind. His Alaskan roommate invited him to work with him on a fishing boat in Alaska for the summer to make a great deal of money. He was prevented from boarding a plane to Alaska, and the FBI explained to him that he was on the No Fly List. He became depressed, slept a lot, and found life meaningless. Within two weeks, while he was in this vulnerable state, two undercover FBI special agents contacted him and suggested they all together carry an attack in the United States—a typical sting operation. He reluctantly accepted, and the two FBI agents guided him in attempting to bomb a Christmas tree lighting ceremony in Portland's main square. Being put on the No Fly List made Mohamud vulnerable to a pitch for engaging in political violence and increased his probability of becoming a threat to the United States— under FBI guidance.[36]

Protection of the United States and civil aviation is obviously vital in our modern world. The government will be able to do so effectively only if it grasps that the assessment process for nominating people to the No Fly and Selectee Lists (and the new Expanded Selectee List that includes even weaker criteria for inclusion than these two lists)[37] is a judgment based on changing conditional probability. The failure to understand the Bayesian nature of the watchlists nominating process results in the dismal performance of the No Fly and Selectee Lists in protecting the homeland from US persons. Given the very low base rate of global neojihadi violence in the United States, the probability of detecting a US person turning to political violence based on static derogatory indicators is extremely small. This probability varies constantly with changing conditions and circumstances and must reach a high threshold to justify violating a person's fundamental right to travel and board an airplane. I suspect that such a threshold may be crossed only when it includes sensitive and specific dynamic factors such as planning for an attack, casing a target, getting access to it, getting the funds to carry out the attack, acquiring means of destruction (weapons or material to construct bombs), and executing an attack.

Policies aimed at protecting the public fail because the government misunderstands terrorism and the small scope of the global neojihadi threat in the West. Because of the very high rate of error (false alarms or false positives), despite the government's great efforts to preserve constitutionally protected civil rights, the process of nomination to the No Fly and Selectee Lists is fundamentally flawed. Despite high-level government officials' protests that this process is more than "mere guesses or hunches,"[38] the ritualistic chanting of this mantra does not make these words a reality and conceals an unfulfilled hope, as it appears that nomination to the watchlists is in fact no more than mere guesses or hunches couched in secrecy. Furthermore, dramatic mission creep has expanded the purpose of the two lists from strict protection of civil aviation to preemptive punishment of mostly nonviolent supporters of suspected terrorists. These lists have failed to identify any of the real terrorist threats against the homeland by US persons already in the United States. The rarity of global neojihadi attacks in the United States is not due to the effectiveness of the watchlists but to the fact that so few US persons have turned to this form of political violence and the fact that foreigners trying to fly to the United States after 9/11 came under greater scrutiny.[39]

Chapter 3

Misunderstanding Radicalization

To the public, acts of domestic terrorism defy comprehension. They seem to come out of nowhere, and their indiscriminate nature undermines the sense that we all belong to the same society. Siblings simply do not kill siblings for no reason. How is this possible? To address this question, however, we need to switch from a macroanalysis of terrorism to a microanalysis that combines group dynamics and cognitive processes.

One Man's Terrorist Is Another Man's Freedom Fighter

There is a consensus among scholars that becoming a terrorist is a process, called "radicalization." Before 2005, few scholars wrote about radicalization: most assumed that terrorism was something foreign imported to one's country, like the 9/11 perpetrators. The acts committed by the homegrown London bombers shattered this illusion, and now, radicalization has become an obsession with scholars. Although much has been written about it in the last decade, people still seem to go back to old beliefs and prejudices when trying to understand it. Despite a growing literature, our understanding of this process remains stagnant.[1]

The term "radicalization" has two different meanings. One involves the acquisition of extreme ideas, or cognitive radicalization, and the other refers to the turn to violence, or behavioral radicalization, allegedly based on these extreme ideas. The two are related but quite distinct: many people have so-called extremist ideas, but very few people act on them. My concern is with behavioral radicalization, the actual use of violence, rather than the far more common talk about violence. Talk of using violence does not necessarily lead to action. Very few people talking about violence go on to use it. This very low base rate must be accounted for in our understanding of radicalization.

One problem that has stymied scholars in the field is the lack of an accepted definition of terrorism, and therefore radicalization. Most definitions include political violence[2] but exclude state violence (or repression) and violence at times of war (when any violence is part of the war). Beyond this, definitions run into a conundrum: "One man's terrorist is another man's freedom fighter." Had the word existed then, George Washington would have been a terrorist to King George III but a freedom fighter for rebellious Americans. Nelson Mandela was a terrorist to the government of South Africa but a freedom fighter for much of the world. Categorizing someone as a terrorist or an action as terrorism depends on the categorizer's perspective.

This conundrum shows that perspective is extremely important. Terrorism divides people into two categories: those who view themselves on the side of the "terrorists" and those who view themselves in contrast to them. I define terrorism as *a public's categorization of political violence by nonstate actors during domestic peacetime.* Terrorists are simply people who carry out acts of terrorism, as viewed from an outside and therefore critical perspective. The word expresses the public's disapproval of individuals who commit acts of political violence. The same public may view the same person as a freedom fighter or a terrorist according to which side he is on. For instance, the American public viewed the Afghan Jalaluddin Haqqani as a freedom fighter in the 1980s but as a terrorist in the 2000s for carrying out the exact same violent activities against foreigners and the Afghan government they supported. He was on the American side in the 1980s (a freedom fighter for Americans but a terrorist for Russians) but against it in the 2000s (a terrorist for Americans but a freedom fighter for Afghan rebels). The meaning of the term has now stretched to the point that authoritarian governments label any nonviolent political dissenters as terrorists. Liberal democracies must resist adopting the terminology of these ruthless and brutal tyrants.[3]

This self-reflexive definition solving the terrorist/freedom fighter conundrum does not mean that terrorism is just a label and arbitrary, or that its study is a semantic game. Rather, this self-reflexive definition allows us to transcend the prejudices built into the terminology, which lead us to misunderstanding terrorism. Before I describe the process of someone turning to violence, let me show that a lack of self-awareness of one's perspective on "terrorists" leads to widespread misunderstanding of radicalization.

Chapter 3

Outsiders' Explanations of Radicalization

A common set of explanations, widely shared by the lay public, is based on the view of terrorists as outsiders who don't belong to one's group. When trying to explain an outsider's behavior, we focus on the person rather than the context. It is easy to create a name for a person doing an action: committing a criminal act makes one a criminal; carrying out an act of terrorism makes one a terrorist. However, the circumstances that generate a criminal or terrorist act elude labeling and are ignored by most people. And once a word is created, it defines a category and then acquires a life of its own, with many associations that are immediately activated along with that category. A word like "terrorist" comes fully loaded with emotional associations and preconceived notions about the types of people that constitute such a category. These preconceptions are very difficult to change, requiring a strong cognitive effort to do so.[4] This decontextualized concept of terrorist asserts some stable characteristic or essence of the person, which allegedly drives him or her to commit political violence. This assertion has led to a search for some predisposition to carry out such acts and a set of personal indicators—a profile—that might help detect terrorists before they carry out their acts. As more facts have emerged about the people committing terrorist acts, however, we have learned that terrorists generally had a normal childhood, which did not predict their later turn to terrorism.

This common cognitive bias neglecting contextual factors and reducing actors to stereotypes, driven by simple internal factors such as personality or ideology, is called "the fundamental error of attribution" in social psychol- ⊥ ogy.[5] It takes the politics out of terrorism and reduces it to personal predisposition. Two common explanations from this perspective are that terrorists are either criminals or mentally ill. However, the empirical literature in the field shows that terrorists come from a variety of backgrounds and the vast majority have no criminal history. Likewise, scholars have reached a consensus that terrorists generally do not suffer from any major mental illness and have failed to discover a "terrorist personality."[6] Nevertheless, since there is no other explanation for the decontextualized violent act, lay people and security officials persevere in assuming some sort of predisposition. This misunderstanding about predisposition is very important: it sends many naïve Muslims caught in FBI sting operations to prison for a very long time; the assumption of predisposition is at the core of the federal case law on entrapment. In court, entrapped people's general speech advocating violence is taken to demonstrate a predisposition for specific acts of terrorism, despite the very low base rate from general violent words to specific deeds. This alleged assumption resonates with juries' prejudices and results in conviction.

More sophisticated psychological explanation avoids the mental illness explanation but keeps the personal predisposition thesis. One prominent scholar has proposed two major psychological variants. The first argues that terrorists, like Palestinian terrorists for example, carry out the mission of their parents, which he poetically summarized: "When one has been nursed on the mother's milk of hatred and bitterness, the need for vengeance is bred in the bone."[7] The second argues exactly the opposite—namely, that terrorism is a rebellion against the generation of the terrorists' parents, like that of the 1970s Western leftist revolutionaries.[8] In this dichotomous world, parents have a strong influence on their children's potential for political violence, either positive or negative. However, most empirical studies show that parents' impact on terrorists is not as important as their peers' influence, which is very different from that of their parents.

As an example of this kind of psychological explanation, one of the rare scholars to have actually interviewed unsuccessful suicide bombers compared four Palestinian bombers who tried to kill themselves but failed because of bomb malfunction with 11 would-be bombers who aborted their mission at the last minute. He found that all four true suicide bombers had a dependent/avoidant "personality" as opposed to 6 of the 11 control subjects.[9] However, the evidence shows that the four failed bombers displayed persistent initiative to convince their respective terrorist organizations to take them on as suicide bombers. This type of initiative is not consistent with the behavior of people with a diagnosis of dependent or avoidant personality disorder.[10] In any case, the small numbers involved prevent us from generalizing this finding, which must be considered anecdotal evidence at this point.

Some psychologists have suggested that the primary motivation in the turn to political violence is a quest for personal significance.[11] A historian has even called this desire for self-glorification the Herostratos Syndrome after the man who burned down the Temple of Artemis in ancient Greece just to achieve fame.[12] There is indeed some element of self-glorification in the turn to political violence. Most terrorists feel they are part of a vanguard and that they matter in the larger scheme of things. But these feelings are private, for they are willing to sacrifice themselves anonymously, knowing that their significant act might not bring them glory. My interviews with terrorists show that when such narcissism becomes too blatant, their comrades distance themselves from them. Egotism is frowned upon among terrorists.

A political scientist has postulated some sort of "cognitive opening" as the core dynamic in radicalization, involving a readiness to adopt extremist ideas.[13] However, this poorly defined concept just seems to be a lay understanding that exposure to a dramatic event may quickly change the beliefs of a person. Retrospective reconstructions of one's life story lend themselves to such an abrupt change of ideas, especially when the interviewer is eager to find one and guides the interviewee's narrative. Nevertheless, some vivid experiences do shock some individuals into volunteering to defend victims of egregious aggressions. Videos of victimized people with whom one shares a sense of social identity may trigger this change, as many empirical accounts of terrorists make clear.[14] In this case, this vague "cognitive opening" may be more precisely described as identification with victims, moral outrage at the aggressor, and a desire to do something about the aggression.

Another general explanation from the predisposition perspective is that terrorists are simply guided by wrong ideas; this argument emphasizes the role of ideology as an explanation for perpetrators' behavior.[15] Its proponents point to the hateful discourse of self-appointed "preachers of hate" and Internet proselytizers and stress their importance in "radicalization"—thereby confusing the two meanings of this term. More recently, its advocates have adopted a politically correct phrase to describe their proposed policy to counter radicalization, turning the focus away from Islam—"countering violent extremism," or CVE for short. This popular ideological explanation heralds the Internet as a very important factor in the increase in young Muslims volunteering to join forces with various Islamist groups in Syria or Iraq. There is no doubt that ideology—or "narrative" in the present lexicon of counterterrorism—may play a role in the turn to political violence. This explanation suggests that this narrative on the Internet finds fertile ground in "vulnerable," "naïve," "at risk," and "predisposed" individuals, who fall prey to it. Alarmists claim Daesh is a very technologically savvy enemy organized from the top down and engaged in a huge propaganda campaign to recruit these vulnerable people, waging a virtual fight for their souls.[16] In fact, most people believe that supporters of al Qaeda or Daesh must have something wrong with their thinking to accept its barbarous ideology. At least republicanism, communism, nationalism, socialism, anarchism, or liberation—the respective ideologies of previous terrorist groups—make sense within a Western perspective, but Daesh's ideology seems to be a throwback to medieval times.

There are multiple problems with the ideological explanation. Mere exposure to wrong ideas can explain neither their adoption nor their power to lead people to self-destruction, as is often the case in political violence. Very few people exposed to the jihadist message ever choose to go abroad to fight. This extremely low base rate of radicalization as a result of exposure has usually been explained away by postulating some sort of coercive face-to-face indoctrination. But such coercion is difficult to achieve on the Internet since users can just log off and move on with their lives. This eventually leads to a tautological argument that only naïve people susceptive to the narrative are radicalized, and their radicalization is thus a sign of their susceptibility.

Therefore, the ideological explanation must be linked to some theory of social influence that can account for the fact that only very few adopt this ideology while the vast majority reject it. One such explanation could simply be that the narrative reinforces socialization in the family or at school. But most terrorists did not grow up with violent ideas (except those persecuted minorities in their own homes, like the Palestinians); indeed, such ideas are usually adopted over the strong resistance of their parents and teachers. A different type of socialization is indoctrination, where experienced believers teach this ideology to newcomers. Most lay people find this ideology inherently incredible, and so believe that this process must be far more coercive than simple benign learning in order to force newcomers to adopt these new ideas. Leaving aside the assumption behind this argument that terrorists cannot think for themselves, this brainwashing presumably involves control of rewards and punishments, thus compelling recruits to adopt the new ideas. As mentioned, however, such coercive methods are difficult to carry out on the Internet.

Another possible type of influence is suggestion: particularly vulnerable people fall under the spell of magnetic people, a form of hypnosis. This version implies that naïve and probably ignorant young people become susceptible to the suggestion of charismatic leaders, who transform them into "true believers."[17] This argument attempts to explain mass movements with a potential for political violence like Nazism and Communism: people in crowds regressed to a more primitive state, making them susceptible to suggestion by charismatic leaders,[18] like Hitler, Lenin, or Mao. When evidence failed to detect parental influence in the turn to violence, the scholar who previously preached the importance of that influence revised his theories and argued that terrorists convert to true believers by subordinating their individuality to the group. In this state, they uncritically accept the directives of a "destructive charismatic leader" and follow them as a "moral and . . . sacred obligation."[19] His argument resurrects the century-old suggestibility thesis, whereby charismatic leaders transform suggestible young people into fanatic killers and suicide bombers. But empirical studies have failed to discover any such zombies with little or no free will.[20]

After 9/11, the common assumption was that sinister al Qaeda spotters lurking in the shadows of mosques turned vulnerable ("at risk") Muslims over to recruiters, who indoctrinated them into joining the organization. These spotters/recruiters allegedly formed an organized worldwide "network" ready to pounce on these Muslims and convince them to go to al Qaeda training camps, where their brainwashing would be completed.[21] However, more than a decade of intense search in the United States failed to turn up any spotter/recruiter—except for FBI agents provocateurs.[22]

The Internet has breathed new life into this explanation. The view now is that sophisticated virtual recruiters on Facebook or other social media spot these vulnerable young Muslims and indoctrinate them online. But a clear understanding of the way people use the Internet refutes this assumption of online passivity. People on the Internet are quite active in communicating with others. They turn on their device, log on to their social media, Facebook page, or jihadi websites, and try to reach out to similar others. They self-select to the ideological sites they like, try to make sense of their world, construct meaning from available models, actively shape their lives, and make choices accordingly.

The Internet is also blamed for the increase in lone global neojihadis,[23] apparently because loners communicate with others only online. The argument seems to be that since both the use of the Internet and the number of loners are increasing, there must be a connection between these two phenomena since loners use the Internet. However, no one has proposed any mechanism for the way that the Internet influence neojihadis to turn to violence. None of the above explanations of radicalization seems to account for the rise of the loners.

There is another type of explanation that abandons the quest to discover internal predispositions and instead adopts a strictly behavioral view of terrorists. This view postulates that people are rational actors, behaving in a utilitarian fashion seeking to maximize benefits and avoid costs. In this rational choice theory, terrorist behavior is the observable result of their cost/benefit calculations according to a predetermined set of preferences.[24] This perspective, whose simple assumptions usually allow scientists to precisely calculate probabilities of choices and predict behavior, provides a simple explanation for the adoption of a new ideology: this process is the result of an indoctrination that selectively rewards its acceptance (through the provision of love and inclusion in a desirable group) and punishes its rejection (through ostracism or retribution). Such selective rewards and punishments, however, lose some of their strength over the Internet. Indeed, loners present a challenge to this perspective. Since they are, by definition, loners, there are no others to reward or punish them into believing the wrong ideas, now fashionably labeled "the narrative." Suicide terrorism seems incompatible with this perspective. A person willing to kill himself or herself for a cause is definitely not maximizing his or her self-interest without distorting the notion of self-interest beyond recognition; suicide terrorism violates the assumptions of rational choice theory. Such a person can certainly act rationally, but not within the utilitarian meaning of this perspective.[25]

Suicide terrorists also present a more general set of difficulties for the ideological thesis. What kind of ideas have the strength to convince individuals to kill themselves? While some self-appointed lay experts on Islam claim that the answer lies in Islam itself, this is not credible. More than a billion people believe in Islam and only a few hundred people have committed suicide in a terrorist act. Furthermore, many non-Muslims have also carried out suicide terrorism. So looking for the answer in Islam does not explain why the overwhelming majority of Muslims (a ratio of more than a million to one) do not commit such heinous acts and why non-Muslims do carry them out. The answer must lie beyond the ideas themselves. These advocates are thus forced to revert to one of the psychological explanations described above.

While I am on the topic of Islam, let me address the issue of the al Qaeda/Daesh ideology. Some Muslims, seeing the destruction and oppression in Muslim lands caused by the West, define themselves in contrast to Westerners. They assume that Western destruction is caused by Western culture, which emphasizes individuality and glorifies personal achievement, hedonism, and consumerism.[26] They reject this culture as simply a justification to maintain the status quo that oppresses them. Instead, they adopt the opposite—namely, a stress on community, authenticity, sacrifice, and care found in religious fundamentalism and specifically Pan-Islamism. What Westerners see as suicide bombing, they celebrate as self-sacrifice in defense of their endangered community. There is nothing medieval in their ideology: it is simply a rejection of some of the unattractive elements of Western culture.

In all these explanations of the turn to political violence, outsiders' perspectives predominate, including among social scientists, who are after all part of society and cannot shed their biases when analyzing terrorist behaviors. Very few terrorism scholars have been terrorists themselves—and so terrorism research is an activity of outsiders. Indeed, most researchers approach this subject from a national security or counterterrorism perspective, adopting without question the state categorization of terrorists as hostile out-group members. In defining them as outsiders, scholars adopt outsiders' biases with respect to terrorists. The scientific requirement of approaching an issue in an unbiased way to counter one's unconscious prejudices makes it imperative that scholars adopt a self-reflexive definition of terrorism like the one I suggested earlier. The fact that political violence is one of the most polarizing phenomena that exists makes it all the more crucial to temporarily suspend judgment in order to understand the root of this evil. Inevitable partiality for victims can blind scholars in their quest.

Insiders' Explanations of Radicalization

When terrorists are asked about their use of violence, they first blame it on grievances. This answer fails to satisfy because a huge number of people share the same grievances but only a very few turn to violence. When challenged about this fact, terrorists then refer to the purpose of their acts, which changes according to circumstances. This purpose gives meaning to their deeds. For example, some acted in order to bring certain political grievances to the attention of an audience and raise political consciousness about them. The problem with this explanation is that after the violence, this audience pays no attention to these grievances but instead focuses on its moral outrage over the violence and its effect—namely, the fear and terror they feel. This may well be the fundamental paradox of political violence: it seldom achieves its intended effect—bringing attention to a set of grievances—but focuses attention, including that of scholars, on the violence and its perpetrators and on how they differ from the rest of society. In carrying out political violence, perpetrators see themselves as acting out the norms, values, and meanings of their group, but outside observers only see their acts and construct a stereotypical profile of people who can carry out such acts.

Eventually perpetrators blame circumstances. This is the other side of the fundamental error of attribution. People tend to attribute another person's negative behavior to internal predisposition, often his belief system—an attribution bias. However, they tend to attribute this same negative behavior in themselves to compelling circumstances—the actor-observer bias. Let's extend this tendency to social groups: members identifying with their own group believe their in-group members' negative actions are forced upon them by circumstances, while those of out-group members are due to internal predispositions.

This explanation blaming circumstances captures the dynamic sense of doubt and insecurity that people experience when acting in the midst of history and having to choose between difficult to assess alternatives. There is a strong contrast between those who live history and those who write it. Pundits often reconstruct past events in a simplistic linear post hoc determinism that contrasts with participants' experience of them and difficulty at the time in detecting significant opportunities from a sea of background minutiae. Participants' sense of confusion about the choices open to them is palpable as they try to guess the consequences of their options at the time.[27] Pundits' certainty and linearity can come only retrospectively, when the complexity of circumstances can be reduced to an abstraction about the factors that later emerged as significant. They ignore that the actors had trouble detecting these true signals from all the noise at the time. As outsiders, pundits also ignore the full circumstances of events, especially actors' understanding of how their situation influenced them at the time. Instead, pundits often fall back on using personal factors to explain behavior. Lay people follow this tendency to ignore context and actors' own understanding of how circumstances influenced them in committing violence. Before dismissing this type of explanation as merely a perpetrator's exculpatory justification for his or her crimes, consider that three-quarters of a century of social psychological experiments support perpetrators' insight that circumstances influence behavior far more than internal predisposition.

Circumstances exert strong pressure on people to behave in a certain way. And focusing on political actors' subjectivity and the meaning they attribute to their action necessarily privileges situational explanation. This explanation lumps together grievances, static circumstances, and the dynamics of events. The static dimension captures the structural elements of the context, but the awkwardness of various expressions to describe this context—conjuncture, opportunity structure, demand characteristics of a situation, or affordance[28]—show that we have no real vocabulary to describe it, which often leads us to ignore it when trying to understand violence. Analysis from this perspective includes a dynamic element, as events unfold in a certain way. In trying to apprehend this evolution, an explanation must provide an account of the chain of events as path-dependent, which is how people experience historical events. It is path-dependent because some irreversible events, like homicide, engage people along a path that affects all their later decisions. This implies that any account of radicalization must trace a rigorous chronology of the significant events that affect actors' understanding of their world. Their action in one event becomes a precedent that becomes incorporated in their cognitive repertoire and is easily called back to mind.[29] The cognitive availability of recent events means that people react to them rather than to long past events that are probably forgotten. Too many studies of terrorism collapse time, leading to erroneous causal attribution of behavior to long forgotten events, such as childhood "traumas" or slights to family honor that the child obsessively remembers and seeks to avenge. Such pathological long-term childhood obsessions are rarely the cause of political violence. Empirically, the few cases of murderous obsessions, usually fascination with one's target, were generated in adulthood. In other words, the incorporation of a violent act into one's easily available cognitive repertoire changes things: crossing the threshold of violence changes a group and makes later group violence more likely.

Nevertheless, this explanation with its connotation of strong environmental pressure for a certain behavior is not, by itself, adequate. Large structural factors affect millions of people, but as I have said, only a very few turn to political violence. So this explanation is not specific enough to lead to a full understanding of the process of radicalization. Circumstances are interpreted by actors, and this interpretation is important for understanding the process. And an explanation based on circumstances brings us back to the subjective way people try to make sense of their world and themselves in it. But while we can focus on how political actors conceive of themselves, their friends, and their context, having a conception does not mean that they understand this process of radicalization. Social and cognitive psychology demonstrate that people are often not aware of why they act the way they do. They give post hoc justifications to interviewers that seem to provide a plausible explanation for their past behavior. However, when tested in the rigorous environment of the laboratory, experimental manipulation fails to support most of these explanations as important contributors to their behavior.

The Internet, which challenges authorities' attempts to impose their perspective on a public, may foster radicalization according to this insider's perspective. The Internet is a source of information that escapes control by authorities and provides an alternate set of events to which militants react. Militants and society rely on separate sources of information focusing on different events according to their respective priorities and assumptions about the world. Militants try to make sense of events ignored by mainstream media through discussions with their peers, often on the Internet, which expands their access to relevant information. In a process of self-selection, militant websites may also nurture and reinforce a strongly atypical view of the world, which increases the gap between militants' understanding of a situation and the rest of society's understanding of it. Each group condemns the other as biased, because each views and interprets different events or sometimes even the same event from its own perspective. The use of the Internet exacerbates this mutual incomprehension between terrorists and society.

Insiders' explanations of their radicalization focus almost exclusively on context. Half a century ago, a scientific attempt to provide a structural explanation of why men rebel stressed relative deprivation, which leads to frustration, aggression, and rebellion, and supported this theory with large cross-country correlations.[30] Ironically, the publication of this thesis coincided with worldwide student rebellions in which many people turning to political violence were the children of elites of their respective countries and did not experience relative deprivation in any meaningful sense of the term.[31] The source of their frustration, if any, was not relative deprivation, and their frustration was not the cause of their aggression. These points limit the usefulness of this explanation as a mechanism of radicalization. The present wave of global neojihadi violence also undermines this argument, since militants are attracted to struggles in distant Muslim lands. Their own relative deprivation in their own country could not have motivated them in adopting a foreign cause.

Another more sophisticated type of structural explanation for the turn to violence inspired by the mass student protests of the 1960s in the West is social movement theory, which tries to account not for violence per se but for large-scale political protest, of which violence is just one aspect. It focuses on mobilization to social movements, which it explains through the efforts of social movement organizations that make resources available for potential members to join.[32] However, in any large demonstration, the majority of protesters are not part of a protest organization—radicalization without organization—and therefore not much influenced by its resources to recruit them into mass protest. Recent social movement theory focuses almost exclusively on impersonal mechanisms that seem to negate the personal agency of the protesters, as if they were mindless robots mechanically following utilitarian cost/benefit schedules.[33] Any explanation of the turn to political violence must breathe life back into this process and recapture the fact that it is a human process, filled with emotion, sacrifice, and blood—which is one of the reasons it is so fascinating. To put people squarely back in the middle of the process of mobilization, a sociological history of the civil rights struggle argued that awareness of expanding political opportunities for protest transformed protesters' consciousness into "cognitive liberation," which resulted in collective action.[34] Another model of mobilization into high-risk activism based on an analysis of the famous 1964 Freedom Summer voter registration drive in Mississippi showed that participation in that dangerous activity had a lifetime influence on the self-identity of participants.[35] However, it would be unwise to extrapolate from a model built on militantly nonviolent subjects to explain the turn to political violence.

In the effort to explain radicalization that leads to political violence, an important insight has emerged from the intelligence community based on the social movement perspective. Government analysts were faced with requests from the field to help distinguish the very few true positives, people who later turn to violence, from the overwhelming majority of false positives, people who brag on the Internet and pretend that they are tough and dangerous but, in fact, just talk, talk, talk—and do nothing. This disparity between the great numbers of "wannabes" and the rarity of violence has generated a consensus in government agencies around a two-step model of the turn to violence. The first step is joining a political protest community, which the government calls radicalization, and the second is the actual turn to violence, which it calls mobilization (to action). (These labels, however, have created confusion within academia, which, following social movement theory, calls the act of joining a political protest community mobilization.) The government's hope is that in cases of true positives, genuine militants give off detectable signature words and behaviors that predict their turn to violence, but to my knowledge, no government agency has reached a consensus about these indicators or tested their sensitivity or specificity.[36]

None of the above perspectives has generated an adequate explanation for the actual turn to political violence. This is the subject of the next chapter.

Chapter 4

Militants in Context

A Model of the Turn to Political Violence

Insiders' or outsiders' perspectives do not generate satisfying explanations of the turn to political violence, as we have seen. There is a third set of explanations for this turn, which transcends these perspectives and studies people in context. Half a century ago, social psychological experiments on conformity[1] and obedience[2] showed how easily people fell under the influence of a small group and would kill subjects when urged to do so by scientific authority. Another experiment demonstrated the power of randomly assigned social roles in transforming normal young men into sadistic prison guards or emotionally broken prisoners.[3] These experiments show the power of situations to dramatically affect behavior without actors even being aware of the subtle experimental manipulations of their environment.[4] Building on these findings, several scholars synthesized linear mechanisms of radicalization, but provide only anecdotal evidence for their respective models.[5]

The context of the process of turning to political violence is a conflict between protesters and the rest of society, especially state agents. Some scholars have called this conflictual context "jujitsu politics,"[6] and the result of its escalation is violence.[7] Within this context, some scholars argue that the process of radicalization consists of a combination of five individual and four group mechanisms. The individual mechanisms—personal grievance, "slippery slope," love, risk and status, and "unfreezing"— are normal psychological processes. ("Slippery slope" is just the idea that a small step may lead to a larger one. "Unfreezing" is simply changing one's mind—unfreezing one's old ideas, developing new ideas, and refreezing the new ones—and is equivalent to the concept of "cognitive opening" described in the previous chapter but without the need of any dramatic incident.) The four group processes—group grievance, polarization, competition, and isolation—are also fairly normal. The weakness of this list is that it is ad hoc, based on anecdotal and selective confirmatory evidence, and that these mechanisms, either singly or in combination, are neither necessary nor sufficient to bring about violence.[8] Since they are ubiquitous mechanisms, their detection lacks specificity. Nor do we know their sensitivity in the process of turning violent, which may very well occur without any of them. These drawbacks limit the usefulness of this list.

Any conflict forces the people involved to identify with one side or the other. Recently, Dutch scholars have put social identity at the center of the process of turning politically violent. Blending self-categorization (to be explained in the next paragraph) and social movement perspectives, they argue that there is no radicalization without identification.[9] They anchor their concept of identity in self-categorization theory rather than clinical psychology, which cannot explain intense immersion in a collective identity except as a pathological process.[10] Their perspective shares the same social psychological and cognitive foundation that frames the model I propose for the turn to political violence.

Like many developments in social psychology, self-categorization, or its parent, the social identity perspective, began as an attempt to understand the Holocaust.[11] This perspective derives from the work of Henri Tajfel, a Polish Jew who had immigrated to France and fought the Nazis. He was captured and survived a series of prisoner-of-war camps in Germany. After liberation, he dedicated his life to studying what had made the Holocaust possible. In examining the nature of prejudice and intergroup relations, he and his student John Turner investigated how people categorized themselves into different groups and discovered that this simple process of categorization was enough to lead to prejudice—namely, in-group favoritism and out-group denigration.[12]

Categorization is a quick, natural, associative, emotional, effortless, and automatic process of simplifying our environment in order to make sense of it by creating categories based on common perceived characteristics.[13] The way we think about ourselves varies according to what is significant to us in a particular context, which determines our level of abstraction: we are human beings in contrast to animals, members of a group in contrast to another group, or individuals in contrast to others within our group. For example, we see ourselves as part of the human race when faced with a natural catastrophe like an earthquake; as part of a nation in the context of international arenas of competition like sport, war, or trade; as part of a group defined by race, religion, gender, or citizenship status in the context of national comparison; or simply as an individual in comparison to other individuals. Our sense of self is fluid and varies according to relevant comparisons, giving us multiple competing social identities. There is nothing like an existential threat against one of them to bring its salience to the fore. An outside attack on Americans, because we are Americans, makes our identity as Americans extremely relevant. Likewise, an attack on Muslims by Westerners makes a Muslim identity in contrast to the West especially salient. In terrorism research, this process centers on self-categorization in contrast to perceived enemies, of ourselves in contrast to terrorists, or for global neojihadis in contrast to Western enemies.

Self-categorization is what makes collective behavior possible. Even loners who commit terrorist acts do so because they imagine themselves to be members of a larger social category: "anarchists," "liberators," "defenders of the constitution or unborn babies," "jihadis," or any member of a vanguard striking out against relevant contrasting out-groups in the name of some virtue. They view themselves as interchangeable members of their social group: one's own personal and individual identity does not come to mind since it is not relevant in that situation. Like athletes during a game, members think of themselves as teammates, not individuals. They become depersonalized: as team members, it is more important for their team to win than it is for them to pad their personal statistics. This process of depersonalization—being a team member rather than an individual player—makes group phenomena possible.[14] This relative neglect of individual in favor of group identity is a natural process that all of us experience when immersed in events as sports fans or patriots.[15] In-group members are teammates and individuals only within the context of the group.

Likewise, opponents are viewed not as individual players but as stereotypical members of the contrasting team or out-group. Self-categorization glosses over intragroup differences and sharpens intergroup differences. This accentuation of in-group similarity and out-group differences simplifies social reality into clear, concise, and manageable categories.[16] In erasing out-group members' individual differences, self-categorization reduces them to one-dimensional characters. This dehumanization may be necessary as a mechanism of moral disengagement to carry out political violence.[17] Self-categorization theory implies that this dehumanization of out-group members is natural and automatic as part of the categorization process. There is no need for any additional desensitization, indoctrination, or brainwashing for this to occur.

People engage in *political* violence not for personal motives, but for group motives. Any threat or injury to another group member is viewed and felt as a threat or injury to oneself, just as any negative turn of events for a sports team is experienced as negative by each team member. This is not a pathological process of losing one's own identity and mysteriously merging with that of the group. It is not indicative of a "true believer" or "weak personality" or some sort of brainwashing. It is not conformity, compliance, or obedience. It is a normal, natural, automatic, and direct consequence of the everyday process of categorizing oneself as a member of a group: within this context, one's identity is the group identity.

This shift from individual to social identification underlies the social identity perspective. This shared social identity both creates and is created by the in-group. And once this sense of shared social identity is established, we see events in the world in terms of their significance for us as group members rather than their implications for us as individuals. A shared social identity also transforms the relationship among members of an in-group to enable coordinated and effective collective action: When we view others as belonging to our group, we are more likely to trust, respect, and cooperate with them; seek out agreement and coordinate with them; give them help; and develop a feeling of group belonging. Shared social identity makes collective behavior possible.[18]

Social categories are not fixed, absolute properties of the observer but are relative, fluid, and context dependent.[19] Activation of a particular category is contextual: it reflects the relevant concern at the time and conforms to the three principles of meta-contrast, availability, and fitness to this context.[20] As I pointed out above, individuals have multiple social identities. Perceived out-group aggression against one of them immediately increases its salience and importance to us. People self-categorize within a particular group when, in a given situation, they have more in common with other in-group members than with the rest of the population. This automatic parsing out of the social world is called the meta-contrast principle, which predicts that we lump people into a single group when individual differences within that in-group are less significant than the differences between in-group and out-group members in a given context.[21] Self-categorization is always in contrast to an out-group. Situations activate the social identity that accentuates in-group similarities and out-group differences to simplify our social world and help us navigate it more easily. This self-categorization is also facilitated by the easy availability of a social category in our cognitive repertoire.[22] And this carving of the social world into given categories must fit the categorizer's understanding of the world.

Activation of a Politicized Social Identity, Creating an Imagined Community

The first step in the turn to political violence according to the model presented here consists of the activation of a politicized social identity, which generates an imagined political protest community. In the context of an escalating conflict with an out-group (often the state), disillusionment with peaceful protest, and moral outrage at out-group aggression, some militants start thinking of themselves as soldiers protecting their political community. This second self-categorization, into a martial social identity, leads a few to turn to violence in defense of their imagined community. In the following sections, I describe the activation of a politicized social identity and the creation of an imagined discursive political protest community. I then show how the social identity perspective implies a counterintuitive theory of social influence and group dynamics.

Politically violent actors did not always view themselves as political. A politicized social identity is activated and a vague and diffuse political community materializes when a serious political grievance divides people into two contrasting sides. For instance, people with a nonpolitical grievance like students, workers, or citizens gathering for a peaceful demonstration become political when the state intervenes to repress their demonstration with violence. The original grievance loses its importance in the face of violence and activates a politicized social identity in contrast to the state. This aggression against a group, such as using the police to crush a peaceful crowd, shocks potential members of a group into experiencing the attack not as neutral observers but as threatened members of this group. Mass media—and now especially the Internet— facilitate identification with victims abroad. Most global neojihadis I interviewed attributed their politicization to watching videos of slaughtered Muslims in distant lands. Most were not politicized before watching a screening of atrocities committed against Muslims at a meeting or now more commonly watching these videos on their own online. What they saw outraged them and activated self-categorization into an imagined community, which included these victims and which was in contrast with the states committing these atrocities. This self-categorization into a politicized social identity transforms the personal into the political. It does not necessarily involve any ideology, religion, or ethnicity though they may be part of one's social identity. The Internet makes it much easier to identify with victims abroad based on a commonality, such as ethnicity or religion. When Western powers bomb Muslims in the Middle East, Muslims elsewhere may identify with the victims and become politicized.

We cannot analyze political violence out of context, without looking at out-group intervention, because political actors define themselves in comparison to this out-group and their actions acquire meaning only in the context of its behavior. Any study of political violence thus must be dialectical: it must include both actors and their contrasting out-group. Self-motivated individuals insensitive to their social context suffer from mental disorder, for lack of responsiveness to social cues is part of the definition of such illness. Political assassins whose mental disorder is the major contributor to their act have existed throughout history and act alone because their illness isolates them from others. They can be dangerous, especially when they are able to function socially and are not institutionalized. However, their violence is not carried out in the name of a political community and has no internal political meaning despite its political consequences. In all other cases, it is impossible to understand the turn to political violence without taking into account out-group activity. The way political challengers make sense of this danse macabre with out-group members, often agents of the state, contributes to their turn to political violence.

The collection of people with a common sense of politicized social identity forms an active political protest community of meaning. It is an imagined community, in the same sense that a nation is, as each of its members imagines that he or she shares something in common with other members of this community.[23] Over time, this community evolves and adopts specific symbols and vocabulary, manners of speaking, shared ways of thinking and feeling about the world, common rituals, preferred references and standards, dress codes, diets, types of relationships, and ways of behaving amounting to a lifestyle, deepening its members' commitment. In short, this discursive political protest community often becomes a counterculture.

Its members are involved in a spectrum of political activities, which may include writing, discussions with intimate circles of friends and with strangers in public spaces, formal meetings, proselytism, demonstrations, civil disobedience, strikes, disruptions, confrontations, and riots. The magic ingredient that makes all these activities possible are constant ongoing discussions, uniting the participants into a large discursive community. It is through discussion that political activists learn about current events and the fate of their friends, encounter new ideas, and develop a specific understanding of the world around them.

Before the age of the Internet, many of these activists expanded their small face-to-face communities through writing letters to each other and putting out newsletters, telling their followers about relevant and significant events, new ideas, and social meetings. These discursive activities forged a sense of social identity among the writers, subscribers, and readers. Members of this epistolary network met frequently for political discussion and social activities, which fostered strong emotional bonds of friendship. People drifted in and out of this nascent community, which was amorphous and fluid, with fuzzy and porous boundaries. These individuals became a community when they started thinking of themselves as members of a community as such. This evolution required the intense efforts of some individuals, who helped shape and structure this loose assortment of people.

The Internet makes identification with small, bizarre, or foreign communities much easier and facilitates the emergence of imagined virtual discursive communities. New technology and social media enable self-categorization with members of listservs or websites, friends on Facebook, and followers on Twitter. Internet pals inform each other about new developments relevant for their virtual groups, especially common threats, dangers and aggressions against them. The extent of these virtual imagined political communities, which are quite real, bears no relationship to the size of actual organizations representing them in the physical world. As a result, imagined communities around the world may grow while their representative organizations are physically destroyed. The physical and imagined communities must not be confused, as the press and governments often do.

At present, the imagined global neojihadi community, the *ummah* (the *ummah* is actually the worldwide Muslim community but global neojihadis claim that they represent it), seems to be growing in Western countries while its most prominent representative organizations, al Qaeda and Daesh, are physically shrinking in the Middle East. Most pundits assume that there is a direct link between those identifying with Daesh in the West and Daesh the organization. They label attacks in the West carried out by Daesh sympathizers on the group's behalf but with no connection to it as Daesh attacks. This creates confusion in the mind of the public: is Daesh growing or shrinking? As shown previously, this confusion is identical to what happened to al Qaeda and its political community ten years ago: while al Qaeda was being eliminated in Afghanistan and Pakistan, homegrown attacks disconnected from the group but carried out on its behalf grew in the West. So far, there has not been any link between any US homegrown plots carried out on behalf of Daesh and Daesh itself, including the December 2015 San Bernardino and June 2016 Orlando mass murders. This is not true for Europe, as returnees from Syria with links to Daesh members have carried out coordinated raids, the most devastating of which were the November 2015 mass murders around Paris and the March 2016 bombings in Brussels.

This analysis challenges two common Western governmental assumptions about Daesh. The first is that the dramatic growth of the Daesh imagined community in the West and the travel of Western sympathizers to fight in Syria/Iraq on behalf of Daesh are the result of a very sophisticated propaganda campaign orchestrated by Daesh. Certainly, Daesh does have a very active propaganda branch, but it does not account for this online success. Some of the most active propagandists on behalf of Daesh are Western sympathizers, who retweet messages and videos favorable to Daesh, without Daesh leadership being aware of them. These online jihadis act on their own initiatives. States such as the United States try to counter the "Daesh narrative" by broadcasting refutations of Daesh claims. These are not likely to succeed. News is not neutral but interpreted through the prism of one's social identity; it acquires different meanings for different groups. Al Qaeda members celebrated 9/11 as a great victory and a source of great pride, while Americans saw it as a great tragedy and a source of moral outrage. In a deeply polarizing subject like terrorism, facts are vigorously contested. To Daesh sympathizers, facts broadcast by the United States are simply viewed as incredible spin. Only news coming from their own community appears credible, and information not consistent with their self-categorization is usually ignored.

A more credible counter source for them would be former comrades, who have gone to fight for the *ummah* but were disappointed or revolted by what they saw from Daesh on the ground and returned home. But most Western countries, with very few exceptions, criminalize these returnees and imprison them, preventing them from warning off other Daesh sympathizers at home. These credible voices in the West should be amplified instead of silenced. Although several Western intelligence agencies understand this, politicians prevent them from using these returnees in a sophisticated counterpropaganda campaign because of their fear that one of these returnees may attack the West at home on their watch. Risk-averse politicians prefer appearing "tough on terrorism" to effectively combating it at home.

A second assumption is that since there is an alleged link between foreign terrorist organizations and domestic terrorists, the way to fight this campaign of violence at home is to destroy the organization abroad: "Let's bomb them there so we don't have to fight them here." Of course, some global neojihadi attacks involve members who have gone abroad to fight and received help from these organizations, like Daesh, before returning home. Eliminating Daesh will stop these attacks. However, the vast majority of global neojihadi attacks are homegrown, without any actual link, physical or virtual, to global neojihadi organizations, whether al Qaeda or Daesh. Bombing them abroad inevitably results in civilian deaths, which may not only expand the imagined community at home but also inspire attacks at home, as described later.

The concept of an imagined community also explains the phenomenon of loners. They are loners only in the physical sense; in reality, they are part of this imagined group. They are physically alone in plotting or carrying out their attacks, but they self-categorize as members of this community and often interact with it online. The Internet now makes it easier for members of a virtual community who are physically alone to plot and carry out such attacks. However, this is not a new phenomenon. Loners have carried out the majority of terrorist attacks in the past two centuries in the West.

An important characteristic of imagined communities is that when people adopt a particular social identity, they seek to discover the meanings and norms associated with their new social category (i.e., "warriors don't do this") and try to follow them. And they define their category not in terms of criteria but in terms of its representative members,[24] its prototypes, who are most similar to other in-group members *and* most different from out-group members. This thinking in terms of prototypes means that the boundaries of members' categories are not set in stone but change with the community's most representative element, which varies according to its comparative context. A category is a fuzzy set with elastic and permeable boundaries.[25] This feature of social identity should not be surprising. As I pointed out earlier, we all belong to multiple social groups—being parent, spouse, worker, voter, or member of a racial or religious category, for example. This means that how we perceive events and behave will vary from context to context, as different social identities and their inherent norms become salient.[26] As the best representation of what it means to be a group member, prototypes exert strong influence on other in-group members. The views, actions, and feelings of a prototype shape group norms. When ordinary members do not grasp the meaning of a situation or know which norms are supposed to guide them, they seek out the prototypes for help. People viewed as prototypical members provide these meanings and guidance for the rest to adopt and act out, either explicitly through their words or implicitly through their actions. As members think, feel, and act to conform to their prototype, these thoughts, feelings, and behaviors become the group norms. In becoming models for others to emulate, prototypes thus create the group's norms.

Effective leaders turn group members into dedicated actors, who want to do what the group would like them to do because it is who they are. There is no need for extrinsic rewards for doing what members believe and feel should be done in the first place after they have adopted these beliefs and feelings from the most prototypical members. In violent political groups, members carry out acts of political violence because they want to do it, not because they are forced or ordered to so. There is no brainwashing or mysterious process of radicalization. They just act out their social identity, like soldiers carrying out violence because that is what soldiers do, and not because of their need for approval, fear of sanction, or group pressure to conform. Note, though, that the beliefs, desires, and feelings embedded in their social identity vary according to the context, especially who the salient out-group is and how the in-group perceives it.[27]

In an informal group where no outside force can impose leadership, potential leaders need to be viewed as champions for the group, acting on its behalf, which implies trustworthiness and fairness toward in-group members. Indeed, leaders' use of force to impose their will on subordinates is a failure of their social influence as prototypes to elicit their desired actions. This is often the result of too much blatant self-interest or self-promotion, which discredits them in the eyes of their comrades, undermines their appeal as sources of inspiration and displaces them as prototypes of their group. True leadership is the exercise of social influence from being a prototype as opposed to ordering people around even if allowed by one's legitimate authority. This is especially true in loose informal groups like violent political groups where formal authority is lacking. True leaders also make other group members feel important and convince them that being part of the group matters and what they do is very significant.[28] Political protest may be a high-risk enterprise, especially where states are very hostile to dissidents. All violent political actors I interviewed were willing to sacrifice their lives for their comrades and cause without hesitation. They wanted to do something significant with their lives before they died and were ready to go down in a blaze of glory.[29] Self-sacrifice for the group reaches its ultimate expression with suicide bombers. These militants actually want to sacrifice themselves; they are not coerced to do so through cynical manipulation by their leaders. Rational choice theory has trouble explaining this finding since self-sacrifice does not benefit the individual.[30]

Political protest communities do not emerge by themselves. They are created through the intense efforts of political organizers, who craft a new sense of social identity in a potential constituency within a political context that makes this identity relevant. Leaders cannot be too far ahead of or behind their constituencies. Thus different evolutionary phases of a community may call for different types of prototypes. Early in its formation, potential members attempt to distinguish themselves from others in a wider group and intellectuals play a prominent role in this definitional task. When it is time to carry out its mission, organizers come to the fore and leave intellectuals behind. The technical problems of carrying out violent attacks, such as the manufacture of weapons, may lead technicians to displace organizers. Thus the context and the task of a group elevate different types of members into positions of prominence.

Political protest communities often evolve into a rejection of mainstream culture and norms, which rebels view as hypocritical and decadent. Such a critique is easy to formulate, since all societies inevitably breed some degree of social injustice, which is either glossed over by elites or justified in self-serving terms. This critique elicits a backlash against the protest community from mainstream society adopting the prevailing social ideology of the elites. The rest of society sees the rebels as traitors, betraying society. The triumph of nationalism in the Western world made people in a given country believe that they all belonged to the same imagined in-group, the nation. By challenging the social foundations of this in-group, rebels are seen as deviant in their own society. It is easy to believe that rebels' betrayal is due to a secret allegiance to a foreign entity, hence the constant search for a foreign and international hand. This sense of betrayal of the community has several implications. Society and its state agents are typically disproportionally hostile to these rebels, an attitude in the case of terrorists sanctioned in the widespread terrorist enhanced legal punishments in Western modern jurisprudence. Patriotic hostility toward domestic rebels in general is also usually greater than that felt toward similarly critical foreigners. Other in-group members subject deviant members to greater denigration and rejection than comparable out-group members and punish them disproportionately for acts committed against the in-group. This greater hostility to traitors is called the "black sheep effect," whereby political crimes are more severely punished than common crimes.[31]

The danger they face from the rest of society contributes to politically violent actors' feeling of being special, part of a vanguard trying to change their societies. Their dangerous mission gives them a sense of pride. An unanticipated success, like an effective demonstration, intensifies this feeling. When others validate the emotion, it becomes even more attractive to be part of the dissident community. When this community is viewed as special and prestigious, with likeable members, the quality of the companionship becomes a major attraction for potential constituents. A pleasant sense of belonging to an attractive group helps maintain a strong sense of social identity and faith in its ideology. As successful churches have long understood, a very active social community helps maintain faith in the group's beliefs.

This type of community attracts new members, who want to become part of it, to be part of the action. They join relatives or friends who are already members of this community. Indeed, joining such informal groups mostly occurs through preexisting friendship and kinship.[32] Unlike religious cults, which proselytize with active recruitment campaigns, violent political groups do not recruit passive or reluctant strangers. All the protesters I interviewed were active, in apparent control of their actions and guided by their sense of shared social identity. They did not see themselves as vulnerable to some ideology or at risk or brainwashed into joining or participating. They were attracted by the rebels' style, which they found cool or chic, and volunteered to join them to be part of this flamboyant community, different and more interesting for young adults than their mundane mainstream society. Out-group members postulate an active recruitment process because they cannot understand how people can willingly join such communities that are hostile to the state and hold extreme beliefs. Newcomers join a political protest community because of their identification with in-group victims and attraction to the rebels' panache. Their entry into this community is facilitated by friends or relatives.

The emergence of such an imagined political discursive protest community through shared self-categorization leads to activities on a continuum of intensity, ranging from nominal participation to complete and exclusive dedication of one's time and efforts. Progression along this continuum of intensity deepens the members' sense of shared social identities and further commits them to this community. With its poorly demarcated and permeable borders, it expands or contracts according to the political context, which influences the extent and intensity of activities. This amorphous, pulsating, internally fluid community of a loose unstable network of people is akin to a social blob. The nodes, or people, of this network are not stable entities, since the activation of shared social identity at a given time depends on salient contextual events, mostly the action of relevant out-groups at that time. Nor are their links or relationships stable; friendships of varying intensity are constantly formed and broken according to their respective rhythms. Social identities and networks evolve over time, and a relationship at a given time often changes later on. This lack of stability in nodes and edges greatly limits the usefulness of social network analysis as a tool for understanding political protest communities.

Emergence of Political Violence

Up to this point, the imagined political protest community I have traced is still not violent. Many pundits and state officials lumping together cognitive and behavioral radicalization mistake this peaceful community for a violent "bunch of guys." The vast majority of political protesters are not violent, in spite of aggressive words reflective of their anger at the state, and most even reject violence. Three additional conditions may turn a few to violence: escalation of hostility between the state and their community, which includes a cumulative radicalization of discourse; their disillusionment with nonviolent legal tactics; and moral outrage at new state aggression against their community. The next three sections address these conditions.

Escalation of Conflict

The turn to violence often results from an escalation in the conflict between political protesters and their salient out-group, often the state. The relationship between state and protesters is dynamic and leads to unexpected developments. An explanation of the turn to violence must take into account this dynamic conflict, which is the context of this process. An explanation that does is more accurate and consistent with the vicissitudes of real life than a deterministic one-sided focus on static factors internal to the protest group (pull factors) or external to it (push factors). Such an explanation also clearly admits the contribution of the state to the emergence of political violence. Since both parties of a conflict are responsible for this escalation, one cannot understand the turn to violence without addressing the state's contribution to this outcome. And with the exception of the work of some rare scholars,[33] this state contribution to the emergence of terrorism has been neglected in the literature. Of course, one can attribute this to the fact that states fund most terrorism research, but this cynical interpretation is not the whole story. Honest scholars in the field self-categorize on the side of the state and, like any other in-group member in a conflict, are blind to their own in-group's contribution to the process and completely blame the out-group for any violence. The state contribution to the process leading to political violence may be the most important still unexplored topic in the field. Acknowledgment of this contribution will help us understand this process and may even start a counter process that can defuse this type of political violence before it erupts.

Participation in political protest may have long-lasting consequences, for it often leads to a long-term change in social identity. People participating in a protest event come to realize that others share their identity, which solidifies it. They often experience a newfound confidence to resist and make claims against the police and other authorities. They feel pride in themselves and their effectiveness in confronting the police, which mobilizes them against police brutality, and may overlook a few instances of violent revenge from their new in-group against the state or the society supporting that state.

As in-group and out-group conflict escalates, there is a shift to extremism. According to the meta-contrast principle, a group's prototypes are its most representative members—that is, those most similar to other group members and most different from the out-group (lumped into one stereotype). As perception of the out-group changes, so do in-group prototypes, who vary as a function of their in-group relationship with its salient out-group. With friendly, cooperative out-groups, advocates of collaboration are prototypical. On the other hand, with hostile and violent out-groups, more belligerent advocates are seen as more prototypical.[34] This shift is very important because prototypes are models generating in-groups norms and exerting strong social influence on other members. A hostile out-group empowers extremist in-group members and endows them with more social influence over the rest of the in-group, thereby shifting the entire in-group to a more extreme position. This hostile context is understood by in-group members as forcing them to adopt a more extreme and radical attitude, as they blame circumstances for their turn to extremism.

The salience of a specific social identity is temporary. Outrage activating a politicized social identity fades with time, and people move on. In a liberal democracy, the boundaries of a political protest community are porous since peaceful political dissent is tolerated. In contrast, autocratic regimes do not tolerate political dissent and punish even temporary protest. In this case, the state determines the boundary of the protest community by closing off the possibility of the dissenter's return to normal life. By punishing dissidents severely and bestowing on them a permanent outlaw status, autocratic states endow extremists with more social influence within the dissident community. Some of its members therefore turn to violence for self and group protection. By treating peaceful protesters as dangerous, autocratic states force dissidents to either submit to punishment or turn to self-defense and violence in a self-fulfilling prophecy.

In a liberal democracy, dissent is supposed to be tolerated, but the state can apply pressure on protesters in more subtle ways and close off their opportunity of returning to normal life. One method is to persecute political protesters by punishing them very harshly for trivial violations that would not ordinarily have elicited an arrest. For instance, police notification to employers of an employee's unpopular political beliefs may get a dissident fired and prevent him or her from living a normal life. Arrest and prosecution of dissidents on trumped up charges may result in either long prison sentences or financial ruin due to legal costs. As a result, those at large and now in judicial limbo are forced to go underground and live a clandestine life, which prevents them from escaping their political protester social identity. Police harassment can also take the form of stop and frisk, constant questioning, brutality, and so forth. All these methods remind dissidents of their outlaw status and social identity, reinforce the image of the hated policeman, and contribute to the escalation of violence between unfairly treated protesters and their enemies, the police.

Most scholars and government officials claim that global neojihadi attacks against the West were unprovoked. They fail to understand that Islamists blame Western states for propping up Middle Eastern tyrants as their main grievance against the West. If Western states then become actively involved in conflicts targeting Muslims or prevent them from defending themselves, militant Islamists consider this involvement an escalation of violence. They enlarge their adversary category from their own tyrants and their states to include belligerent Western states.

Concomitant to the physical escalation of conflict is a rhetorical escalation on both sides. Each group sees its out-group's most extremist voice as most representative of the out-group,[35] ignoring general out-group condemnation of this type of speech while also ignoring its own in-group's violent words. Fueled by sensationalist seeking media, extremist speech predominates as perception of out-group extremism, gives credibility to in-group extreme positions and justifies the group's hatred of its enemy. This vicious cycle of mutual reinforcement of opposite extremes raises the volume of voices for violence in the cacophony of in-group noise. As long as the out-group threat remains imminent and present, in-group moderate voices are muted because they lack credibility in defense of their group. Extremist contenders for group leadership exaggerate the threat and danger to rally neutral members around them and discredit internal rivals as being too soft on the out-group and unable or unwilling to adequately protect the in-group against the out-group.

By mobilizing their group against its enemy, they hope to increase their social influence, which they can wield for their own purposes.[36] They become intolerant of internal challenges in this alleged emergency and accuse these challengers of betraying the group, triggering the black sheep phenomenon.

The dominance of verbal extremism over concrete and reasonable proposals to deal with the situation is important here. Extremist discourse precludes dispassionate discussions in the search for fair and just solutions to a group's grievances. Extremist speakers create a polarized atmosphere, and as they use extremist concepts to interpret their group's experience of reality, they propose extreme solutions. Such speakers take a few incidents out of context and then blow them out of proportion. Violent discourse helps extremists shape how people feel about or make sense of events, thus influencing how they act. This discourse obscures the mutual dynamics that lead to retaliation and self-defense. War metaphors are especially harmful as they imply violent action, justify physical violence, and decrease the threshold for it. In retrospect, the situation is never as dire as portrayed in the speech of extremists nor is the struggle with the out-group as significant as they claim. But extremists come to believe their rhetoric and delude themselves about the grandeur of their fight.

The Internet exacerbates these escalations. Without any obligation to check facts, it amplifies rumors through constant repetition. It allows each polarized side to harden its positions and prevents any dialogue between opposite parties broadcasting their extremist messages. Some social media further aggravate this situation by reducing complex issues to 140 characters. To top it off, the absence of the physical presence of an adversary allows Internet mediated communication to shed the last vestige of civility.

While hate speech must not be equated with violence, this cumulative radicalization of discourse rather than ideology per se favors extreme solutions and encourages violence.[37] These very violent words are often mistaken for violence. However, there is a huge gap between words and deeds. This virulence of discourse from political protesters is mirrored in the speech of champions of the state or society.

Disillusionment with Nonviolent Tactics

Another contributor to violence is disillusionment with the results of nonviolent protest. In a duplication of the famous Stanford Prison Experiment, researchers found that disappointment with the efficacy of one's group led to acceptance of a more efficient but tyrannical leadership.[38] This was mediated by the strength of one's identification with the group. People with a weak sense of social identity with the community are not willing to make any sacrifice for it. They are free riders, letting activists take on all the costs of participation and benefitting from these efforts at no or little cost to themselves.[39] When faced with any adversity or with the inefficacy of the community to bring about reforms, they quickly lose interest, leave the community, and fade from history. In general, members in a declining group either leave it (exit) or voice their discontent (voice) to redress this decline; these two options are mediated by their loyalty to the group.[40] If loyalty is viewed as the strength of one's identification with the group, then those with little or no investment in this community are the ones who exit quickly when faced with the first sign of adversity or disappointment with the community. Vindictive states are counterproductive in preventing these weak protesters from giving up their political social identities and melting back into society.

Moderately committed group members are willing to sacrifice some time, effort, and resources for their community. They can be expected to voice their displeasure at the ineffectiveness of the community to redress group grievances. They complain that what they are doing is ineffective and that leaders "just talk, talk, talk—and nothing happens." Over time, feeling disappointment with the group or confronted with punitive measures from the state, they will also leave the community and fade away, but later than the free riders.

Members who have sacrificed too much to give up their political activism can be expected to persist and even redouble their efforts to negate the decline or ineffectiveness of their group.[41] Within this subset of members willing to sacrifice themselves for the cause, rhetorical escalation convinces a very few that the rules of the political game are unfair and that extralegal forms of protest are necessary. They escalate their activism to include more extreme and perhaps illegal measures. Other members, disillusioned with the inability of the protest community to achieve significant progress in resolving their grievances, let more radical members use more extreme tactics on behalf of their comrades and cause. Some may be willing to join the extremists in their use of violent tactics, fully aware that their sacrifice means imprisonment or even death.

Disillusionment with the gains of a political protest community may explain the common observation that political violence often erupts at the tail end of a legal political protest campaign. When most members exit, a few activists disappointed with the results of a protest campaign escalate to violence in a last ditch effort to redress the original grievances. At the same time, the state, which did not dare crack down on a very large social movement, may decide to do so when the community of protesters shrinks to a more manageable size. This leads to a mutual escalation of violence.

Moral Outrage at State Aggression

Disillusionment, by itself, is usually not enough to turn politicized people to violence. Often there is a triggering incident, an unexpected and egregious act of out-group aggression against the in-group. In a group, all members feel an attack on one is an attack on all, eliciting strong feelings of moral outrage against out-group aggressors and calls for punishment. Emotions play a critical role in the turn to political violence.[42]

Moral violations are of course in the eyes of the beholder. In-group aggression against out-group members does not cause outrage in the in-group because in-group members see the result of their own aggression with indifference as "collateral damage," either necessary in the struggle against the out-group or accidental. They dismiss such collateral damage as unfortunate, because it was not intended in the first place. It generates a feeling of indifference but no guilt among them. Out-group members, of course, feel the full brunt of this aggression and cannot dismiss it in such a casual way. Rather, they do not believe it was an accident and see it as the goal or intention of the aggression. Social events are seldom neutral: people interpret and react to them through the prism of their social identity.

Note that in-groups and out-groups do not constitute the entire social realm. Third parties who are, at least initially, not members of either the in-group or the out-group do exist, but they are not an undifferentiated mass. Many have a latent social identity with one or the other group, and as this social identity is made salient through the aggression, it transforms them into either in-group or out-group sympathizers or even members. The aggression politicizes them and makes them imagine that they are part of an active political community. Americans in Alabama watching 9/11 on television immediately felt American (rather than Southerners disliking northern Yankees) and took the attacks in the Northeast United States personally as an attack upon themselves. In contrast, some Muslims who strongly identified with Muslim victims of previous Western aggression celebrated the abstract blow against this Western symbol. They did not celebrate the loss of life per se but a symbolic victory against an abstract West with a long history of persecuting them. This does not mean they delighted in the horrendous loss of life; their feelings were a normal result of self-categorization. However, except for extremists, their identification was not strong enough to make them feel that they were part of the militant Islamist social movement. Third parties, not leaning toward one group or the other, find it easier to identify with concrete victims than with members of a mysterious terrorist group. The vividness of victims portrayed as suffering in the mass media facilitates imagining oneself as one of them. This explains the widespread sympathy for Americans in the immediate post-9/11 era, including on the part of most Muslims the world over.

People with conflicting latent social identities may experience a dilemma: dual loyalty to various potential groups is transformed into divided loyalty when these groups are in conflict. For instance, after 9/11, Muslim political activists who self-categorized in contrast to both the West and al Qaeda were torn between their competing social identities. Many avoided this dilemma by denying that Muslims carried out the attacks, a common belief among militant Muslims at the time.

The most egregious aggression against a group is the killing of one of its members, who, in death, becomes a hero or a martyr as he or she is viewed as having been killed for belonging to the group. Those viewed as dying "fairly"—that is, either in combat or by fair execution for crimes committed—are seen as heroes by the in-group. Regardless of their previous backgrounds, their deaths transform them into group prototypes: sources of celebration, inspiration, and emulation for the rest of the group. Their models can influence others in the group to turn to violence to some extent.

Martyrs, however, are different from heroes:[43] their fate is seen as very unfair or disproportionate to what they have done. For in-group members, their undeserved death is the ultimate sacrifice for the group, which instantly endows them with virtue and cleanses their reputation of any previous flaws. They inspire strong motives for action: some members harden their resolve and press forward further along their path to violence. These reactions are not about ideology but about injustice done to the in-group. While heroes become inspirational models to follow, they do not elicit the same moral outrage as martyrs' deaths, which generally push comrades more widely to action.[44] Martyrs are important in the turn to political violence because their deaths cry out for revenge, igniting retaliatory escalation that results in full-blown violence. An unfair murder of an in-group member that goes unpunished by authorities is seen as an egregious attack on the group, rousing members to defend themselves and avenge their martyr. This can quickly degenerate into a cycle of retaliatory violence: revenge for the martyr is met by unfair prosecution fueled by mass hysteria about an exaggerated danger, leading to greater retaliation and so on.

Threats to wipe out a group, disproportionate state punishment against members, and recruitment of spies or traitors undermining a group's social identity are other common causes of moral outrage, leading to violence. In fact, punishment of insider betrayal, as seen in the black sheep effect,[45] is often the first instance of a group crossing the line into violence. Once this internal line is breached, it is much easier to imagine violence against selective out-group members, especially those responsible for the recruitment of the traitor.

Aggression against symbols of one's social identity also elicits moral outrage and violence to avenge this insult, as seen in the global neojihadi wave of attacks against people responsible for the cartoons denigrating the Prophet Muhammad. This is especially so in groups where honor is important.[46] Aggression against social identity symbols, such as burning or debasing flags, crosses, or religious books or drawing insulting caricatures of one's emblematic founder, elicits anger and retaliation as a personal insult would. Criticism of group prototypes or praise of enemy prototypes is also seen as an intentional insult demanding some form of apology or redress.

Out-group aggressions shift in-group perception to a view that the social world is dangerous and the group needs to defend itself. In this atmosphere, any self-defensive action that crosses the threshold of violence may start a slide down the slippery slope to full-scale violence. The pressure to support one's comrades in such a belligerent context may transform single acts of violence into a full campaign of political violence. Crossing the line to violence is important; this crossing is then readily available in the minds of comrades, who may start to view it as legitimate, especially if the state overreacts to this first act of violence. Having acts of violence cognitively available may explain the copycat phenomenon, as many violent acts seem to cluster together. Once the line is crossed, violent action becomes incorporated into the group repertoire of possible political actions and inspires other members to follow suit or escalate.

However, isolated acts of violence are usually not enough, by themselves, to lead to campaigns of violence. For that to happen, moral violations must find the fertile ground of disillusionment with the political protest community's effectiveness. In the context of an escalating conflict with the state, this combination of disillusionment and moral outrage is powerful and leads some of the most dedicated activists to question the use of nonviolent forms of protest, which have resulted only in increased state repression that they cannot prevent through legitimate means. A few exasperated activists, too invested in the community to leave, and tired of "talk, talk, talk," react to the latest outrage with "enough is enough, and we need to do something about it."

Activation of a Martial Social Identity

In the face of mounting out-group threats and attacks, with no legal recourse to prevent or stop them, a few exasperated activists step up and volunteer to defend their imagined community. They now self-categorize as soldiers defending victimized comrades against salient belligerent out-groups. This activation of a martial social identity does not usually come as a conscious epiphany or a gradual evolution from careful reasoning or better understanding of an ideology. Self-categorization is an unconscious process linked to an understanding of the ever-changing in-group/out-group dialectic. Most of the time, there is no key event identifying the precise moment of this self-categorization, but at some point, the actor views himself or herself as a soldier fighting for comrades and cause. The duration of this process may be very short. It is always possible to go into the background of violent individuals and, with the help of hindsight, pick out episodes from childhood as indicative of a personal predisposition to violence. However, such an analysis ignores the overwhelming evidence that simply does not fit into this preconception but rather points to the collective nature of this new, shared social identity.

Chapter 4

All my interviewees believed they were soldiers defending their persecuted community, the *ummah*. I could not elicit precise boundaries between their non-politicized, politicized, and martial social identities, which would have required them to have a degree of self-awareness that they simply did not have. The process of self-categorizing and making sense of the social world is ongoing, as people are always reinterpreting their positions and roles in their changing environments. Picking out a "stage" of this process is arbitrary. Nevertheless, people who have undergone this turn to violence think about it in retrospect as an evolution. There was a period in their lives when they did not think of themselves as soldiers or defenders of the *ummah*, and there was a later period when they did. In retrospect, many attribute this change to specific events, such as watching the mass murder of Muslims, invasion of a Muslim land, unfair prison time, or learning about egregious injustice against comrades.

Emerging violent militants understand and react to key events according to the evolution of their personal and their group's self-concepts, which as I've pointed out is gradual, natural, and largely outside of self-awareness at the time.[47] With some rare exceptions, they generally do not set out to become violent political actors. On the contrary, many start out explicitly rejecting violence, but once they adopt a martial social identity, or the state treats them as violent enemies, they act out their new identities. They start to go on short paramilitary excursions, learn paramilitary skills, practice martial arts, get weapons, take target practice to improve their skills, and so forth. These activities then reinforce their martial social identity.

The use of violence raises the issue of its legitimacy in killing for the cause. Some political activists, endowed with delicate sensibilities, are willing to use violence only if they can sacrifice themselves, rationalizing that they earn the right to kill through their self-sacrifice. Their own death is the price of murder and reestablishes their belief in a just world, balancing the clearly illegal acts they are about to accomplish.[48] However, most violent political actors have no such scruples. Activation of a martial social identity legitimizes political violence: the perpetrators are just soldiers defending their imagined communities. Soldiers are supposed to fight; violence is simply what they do. Self-categorization into a martial social identity means that violence is imminent because people with this social identity are likely to act out who they believe they are. Over time, war metaphors subtly replace self-defense as their frame and guide for action. It is but a small step for soldiers to go from defense to offense (in the name of general defense of their imagined community), from spontaneous self-defense resisting arrest to stopping arrests by deliberately killing those who order them and so on. The logic of war allows for the possibility of going on the attack, and expands violence from the limits of self-defense to offense. Violence becomes justified to gain any advantage over one's enemy and bring about its defeat. War defies self-imposed limits on violence.

There is some debate as to whether this turn to violence is logical or emotional; rational or expressive; deliberate long-term strategy or gut reaction of irrational people. But such debate ignores the findings of recent research. Emotions do not negate rational thinking. Discoveries in the neuro-cognitive basis of moral thinking, in fact, suggest a close integration between cognition and emotion, especially when actions are involved. Brain areas of feelings and thought are closely associated and too intertwined in moral reasoning to be neatly separated, as is so often done in abstract analysis.[49]

As for those people who act on their own as loners or couples, the social identity perspective shows there is nothing about them that warrants a special label, like lone wolf. They simply act out their sense of shared martial social identity. Indeed, the social identity perspective emerged from an explanation of behavior in studies of "minimal groups." These "groups" were not groups at all but consisted of just a single individual randomly assigned to a category, which in the subject's mind became an imagined in-group. These loners demonstrated social biases in favor of their imagined group and discrimination against salient out-groups. Since each was the only member of this imagined group, there was of course no interaction with other members of the category. Self-categorization into a group in order to make sense of the world is enough to elicit the social dynamics of intergroup behavior.[50] Loners are simply examples of this self-categorization, just like any other real group members.

This new martial self-categorization indicates a willingness to sacrifice one's life for comrades and the cause. Some of my interviewees explicitly stated that they wanted to do something significant with their lives before they died. They believed that fighting back would reestablish pride and self-esteem in a discouraged and disillusioned *ummah*.[51] The willingness to sacrifice oneself for a community means that this cause is worth personal risks to the individual and gives meaning to one's life.

Very few group members volunteer to defend their political community; the vast majority take a free ride and let others bear the burden of protecting it.[52] Thus the self-appointed soldiers for their community become frustrated and even angry with other members of their community whom they see as being too resigned to their lot when they do not join the fighters in their new violent enterprise. Their willingness to use violence gradually isolates them from their former comrades, who do not want to get into trouble with the authorities and so avoid these violent militants. At the same time, many former comrades see the fighters' use of violence as undermining and discrediting their common cause and are angry that this violent faction is trying to hijack their movement. In return, the soldiers gradually see their former comrades as wimps, lose their trust in them, and in turn stay away from them. Gradually, they redraw the fuzzy, fluid, and porous boundaries of their imagined community, excluding their former comrades from their new in-group. They gradually expand their out-group enemy from state agents and their allies to include former comrades who reject violence and finally incorporate the population as a whole for its support of the state. For these soldiers, all members of this expanded out-group become legitimate targets of violence. The history of Western political violence shows this evolution from narrowly targeted violence to indiscriminate violence against the general population.

The self-conceived soldiers begin feeling and thinking of themselves as special, different from the rest of their community, believing that they are the vanguard of the revolution, creating history as they go along. Like soldiers everywhere, they develop a strong esprit de corps. The greater the sacrifice, the greater their self-esteem and the closer they feel to each other. Their baptism through risk, hardship, and common experience of violence transforms them. They prefer to associate with other fighters because they feel part of the same high-risk group and do not have to constantly explain themselves, their views, and their actions to outsiders. Just being among like-minded companions—who understand them, accept them for who they are, and share their social identity, beliefs, and fate—is pleasant, comfortable, and relaxing. As the violence builds, members of a violent group end up spending all their time together.

To escape arrest, these self-categorized soldiers go underground. This social isolation limits their exposure to events and to other ideas, feelings, perspectives, and interpretations of the world; without exposure to a wider gamut of ideas, they experience a narrowing of their cognitive horizon,[53] often centered on an obsession with their enemies. They now share this mind-set only with other clandestine companions. They naturally dismiss any critique of violence outside of their in-group as obviously biased. Likewise, they reject any warning about the misuse of violence from former comrades because they feel superior to and believe they know better than these nonviolent protesters do. Their isolation and exclusive intercourse with like-minded extremists lead to mutual approval and reinforcement of their views, feelings, and behavior, validating and hardening their beliefs about the social world and the necessity for violence. And in becoming increasingly isolated, they become more self-referential and develop a private language that soon becomes incomprehensible to outsiders, including former comrades. This narrowing of cognitive horizons gives outsiders the impression that the violent militants are irrational because of the opacity of their beliefs, fanatic because of the strength of these beliefs, and rigid because of their resistance to outside arguments. These adjectives reduce a set of complex group dynamics to personal attributes, fostering the belief that there is something wrong with the thinking of these militants, that they have some sort of pathological hatred.[54]

But as this evolution occurs, violent militants start to convince themselves that violence may bring about reforms or is more widespread than it actually is: they delude themselves that revolution is around the corner in a triumph of wishful thinking over reality. This bizarre groundless optimism probably comes from their constant obsession with revolution, their gradual isolation from the general population, and the narrowing of their cognitive horizons, which leads them to overestimate the popularity of their own beliefs. When the public fails to follow their lead, they turn against the society, which they now view as composed of cowards.

More often than not, the result of their violent campaign brings about the opposite of what they intended, not state concession but further polarization and anger from the general public.[55] As a result, in the larger society, a mirror self-categorization takes place, and violence causes a shift in favor of extremist champions of state repression, who succeed in imposing ever-stronger repressive measures.

Elsewhere,[56] I empirically tested this model both qualitatively and quantitatively on 34 campaigns of political violence, covering more than two centuries, spanning four continents, and including various types of ethnic, sectarian (Christian, Buddhist, and Muslim), and secular violence from all over the political spectrum. The model was strongly supported in terms of both self-categorization into a political protest community and then into soldiers defending it (91 percent of the cases). Escalation of conflict occurred in 71 percent, disillusionment in about 80 percent, and moral outrage in about 70 percent of the cases, respectively. Although no single model can explain the turn to political violence, these empirical findings strongly support this model as a major explanation for the turn to political violence.

The Dynamics of Political Violence

A Bunch of Violent Guys

We can thus see self-appointed soldiers as a bunch of violent guys emerging from the political protest social blob in an informal and gradual process. States, by contrast, have institutions to formally convert civilians into soldiers in a top down process; for political challengers, this transition is generally bottom-up based on self-categorization. This difference has specific consequences for the composition, structure, and dynamics of these violent groups.

The emergence of politically violent groups is not linear but haphazard and difficult to determine in advance because of the contextual contingencies involved. They emerge out of discussions among committed members of the larger community occurring at informal gatherings and now more commonly on the Internet. Their social identity, mutually negotiated through discussions within a specific context, converges around the need to use violence. Such discussions are dangerous, for the state is often vigilant, and therefore take place among trusted friends and relatives, who over time may become a bunch of violent guys. Because this self-selection from networks of friends and relatives results in homogeneous small clusters that are fluid with fuzzy boundaries between them and their original political community, the nascent violent group is difficult to detect from the rest of the community, which explains the usual difficulty states have in identifying all the conspirators in a plot. As we've seen, these boundaries are porous at first, but they harden and become less permeable after states declare those progressing to violence outlaws and prevent them from fading back into society.

These informal clusters are unstable, for they lack top-down authority that can impose a legitimate leader to resolve inevitable internal disputes. Personality conflicts frequently erupt among rivals and threaten to undermine the group's mission. Rivalries often disguise themselves as ideological disputes or degenerate into accusations of betrayal. Most accounts of campaigns of political violence greatly underestimate this instability. History is written retrospectively, starting from the end—the violence—and tracing it back to its origin in a linear fashion. It ignores the many splinter groups that faded into oblivion because they failed to cross the threshold of historical attention and creates a sense of inevitability and determinism for the group whose violence helped it achieve notoriety. Viewed prospectively, all these violent groups were plagued by internal rivalries. Much energy is devoted to these disputes among conspirators, sometimes distracting them from the execution of their plans and at other times, on the contrary, facilitating violence in competition with their rivals.[57] This internal strife is hidden from outsiders, giving violent clusters a deceptive appearance of cohesion. Insiders do not wash their internal laundry in public; and outsiders lump insiders into a single stereotype. In reality, many original members drop out of nascent violent groups to be replaced by militants who are more compatible with the emerging group.

Most often, the group is engaged in constant discussions, with members egging each other on. There usually is no clear leader but an active core, usually two to four prominent members of the informal bunch, who initiate and drive the violent conspiracy. The core is not fixed; rather it evolves according to the dynamics of internal rivalry and the context influencing group prototypes. Thus, contrary to the traditional static view of leadership, this fluid core waxes and wanes according to the dynamics of the context. This explains why it is sometimes very difficult to identify the leader of these informal clusters.

Violent state aggression increases the social influence of emerging violent clusters within their original community. Champions of violence rarely give an ideological reason for their advocacy to comrades in the larger political community. They already share the same ideology, but the active core attributes the necessity for violence to the state escalation of violence against them. This context empowers them with credibility and justifies their violent response to state escalation of conflict. Ideological justifications are usually directed at people outside the larger political protest community.

The willingness of the active core to use violence, become outlaws, and therefore sacrifice themselves for the larger protest community in the context of a belligerent out-group makes them prototypes in this larger community, attracting some new comrades to the cause of violence. These newcomers want to join the violent cluster, and its active core wastes little effort on "recruiting" like-minded and often younger comrades. Newcomers either volunteer eagerly, begging the active core to take them, or simply accept an invitation to join in their violent enterprise. Usually, the active core's views are well known in the larger community, especially to friends and relatives, who often just go along out of solidarity. The expansion of these violent clusters is often based on such preexisting networks of trust, grounded in friendship and kinship. This allows for last minute "recruitment" based on the demands of the operation. There is no need for a prolonged period of development, indoctrination, or brainwashing.

This analysis implies a continuum of commitment and activism in the new violent groups, ranging from a dedicated active core to associates who tag along and finally to peripheral comrades, who might know about the conspiracy and help their violent comrades in minor ways but otherwise do not actively participate in violent operations. What distinguishes the three levels of participation in political violence is that only the active core initiates and drives violent plots; associates are full participants but, on their own, would not have initiated or pushed the plot along; peripheral comrades suspect but do not know the details of the plot. Peripheral members still feel loyalty to and solidarity with their more involved friends or relatives, a solidarity that leads them to help provide shelter, money, and protection by keeping silent. Indeed, in many political communities persecuted by the state, such help is a sacrosanct duty, no questions asked, and cannot be refused to a comrade. These peripheral comrades constitute a large loose network of potential supporters. They may not share a sense of martial social identity and sometimes explicitly reject violence. Nevertheless, they feel they have no choice but to show solidarity with their comrades, despite strong disagreement with them over violence. To complicate this picture further, the degree of participation in political violence is not static. Disproportionate and indiscriminate punishment by the state of low-level support may drive peripheral participants to violence; it may trigger a feeling of moral outrage and activate a new martial social identity in them.

I did not find a violent predisposition in these perpetrators. A few might have previously had violent tendencies, but the vast majority had no previous record of criminal violence, and most were explicitly nonviolent when they originally became politically active. Nevertheless, in the escalation of conflict with the state, they did not hesitate to volunteer to carry out acts of political violence when they became disillusioned with nonviolent tactics and morally outraged at state aggression.

Many political activists over the years have come from families sympathetic to social change. In childhood, they may even have internalized core family values of generosity, fairness, and justice. Many revolutionaries in history were "red diaper babies."[58] However, we cannot draw a straight line between parents' political social identity and that of their children. The children's path to political violence in these cases was not linear, and there was plenty of generational conflict between parents and such children.

Even for red diaper babies, the turn to political violence was quite complex, involving personal confrontation with out-group injustice and aggression. Their core family values made them especially outraged when personally faced with inequity from the out-group. Global neojihadis' path to violence seems even more complicated. Very few were "green diaper babies" and their path to violence went through rebellion against their traditional family values.[59]

There is one important fact to consider about people who become political activists, one that seriously affects their future path: Intense political commitment demands time. This fact has implications for who is likely to become deeply committed and violent. Clearing their schedule is easier for students, the unemployed, or the casually employed. Students are in a time of transition as they leave their families of origin. In a new environment and surrounded by new friends, they are open to new possibilities, young enough to have energy to pursue them and free enough of commitment to sacrifice themselves for friends and ideals. As competing new family commitments or job responsibilities grow, they are no longer as available for political activism. Thus people whose activism becomes their major preoccupation and identity often reject traditional occupations, trades, or professions that cannot accommodate their consuming engagement. They seem comfortable with a sense of indeterminacy toward the future. And when a spouse does not support a militant's new martial identity or discourages involvement in violent activities, the militant usually gives up either the spouse or the violence.

The strong bonds forged in adversity and violence consolidate an "all for one, and one for all" commitment and make for a "band of brothers" unlike any other. Increased personal danger and a shared fate cement their common sense of social identity into strong affective esprit de corps. This natural and automatic affection adds a sense of joy when companions meet, interact, and carry out their activities together. These fraternal bonds demand that they share equally in the risks, costs, and sacrifices experienced by brothers. They want to feel that they are carrying their share of the burdens and dangers and that they are not letting their buddies down. Their fraternal love increases their eagerness to protect and defend endangered brothers, and this makes violence more likely.

Political commitment is not gender specific. Strong mutual emotional feelings of militants, not surprisingly, often lead to sexual bonds among them, which encourage, reinforce, and accelerate their paths to violence. The intensity of the sexual relationships formed in these violent groups is hard to match and is just one illustration of the intense affective bonding among the companions. Not infrequently, lovers are willing to gamble everything to save their mates.

In this context, any attempt to understand out-group members and portray them as anything but pure evil is seen as a betrayal of this strong in-group loyalty. Accusations of sympathy with the out-group immediately follow: "Whose side are you on?" This is also true for society, which, in a mirror self-categorization, feels the same way toward these political challengers. Any attempt to understand challengers' subjectivity is met with cries of betrayal of society. To self-categorized members of society, an attack on their group demands repressive measures. Violent clusters retaliate, eliciting greater state repression and persecution, which leads to greater retaliation in an ever-escalating cycle of mutual violence.

As a "bunch of guys" travels along their path to violence, their activities gradually cross the line into full-fledged illegality. There is a gradual increase in suspicious activities. Conspirators show a keen interest in previous instances of political violence. They read about past attacks or learn chemistry in order to make bombs. They discuss ideas, previous political attacks, and plans for possible attacks of their own. They may practice their skills in laboratories or on camping trips. They show unusual interest in potential targets and start casing them. They need money for their planned operations and raise it through personal income or wealth, solicitation from rich sympathizers, loans, fraud, or robberies. They acquire necessary weapons, ranging from knives to firearms to bomb-making materials. Many realize that an operation may result in their deaths, and record their wills or just say good-bye, partially explaining their upcoming action. Finally, just before executing the operation, they approach their target and change their appearance to blend into their surroundings. At this point, violence is a solid part of their repertoire of political activities, and the turn to political violence has been completed.

Continued Campaigns of Political Violence

For most perpetrators, the first instance of violence is their last, as they are killed or arrested in the process. These single attentats do not evolve into campaigns of violence. For the few others who survive their first attentat, violence acquires an unintended dynamic of its own. Once its threshold is crossed, violence overshadows all other aspects of the group's relation with the outside world. Revolutionary organizations neglect their peaceful social programs of recruiting the masses to their cause. Violence attracts just a few people in society and usually alienates them from the vast majority. When the larger society is unfairly ruled by a small minority easily distinguishable from the rest of society, like foreign colonialists or distinctive ethnic or confessional elites, violence and state retaliation may polarize society, with most viewing the challengers as part of the societal in-group, and supporting their actions against the ruling minority out-group. This case is an exception, however; in the majority of cases, although violence may be emotionally satisfying to counter disillusionment and address moral outrage, it is generally a self-defeating strategy to redress parochial grievances.

Violence is sustained by internal dynamics—namely, the need for leaders to fend off ever more radical rivals and keep up the morale of their subordinates to avoid their discouragement and exit from the movement. Violence corrupts moral values, as all actors cut corners in pursuit of their goals. "It arouses ferocity, develops brutal instincts, awakens evil impulses and prompts acts of disloyalty," asserts the Russian revolutionary Vera Figner. "Humanity and magnanimity are incompatible with it . . . all methods were fair in the war with its antagonist, that here the end justifies the means. At the same time, it created a cult of dynamite and the revolver, and crowned the terrorist with a halo; murder and the scaffold acquired a magnetic charm and attraction for the youth of the land,

and . . . the more oppressive the life around them, the greater was their exaltation at the thought of revolutionary terror."[60]

Challengers' violence brings about an equivalent bloodlust in society and its official agents, who, in this context, no longer view themselves as guardians of societal peace but as avengers of violence's victims (their in-group). Out-group violence shifts social influence to advocates of intense repression and punishment. Their arguments gain popularity with the public, which undergoes a similar shift to extremity. Violence polarizes the social world, hardens the respective belligerents' positions, and minimizes the possibility of political compromise or reconciliation in favor of pure revenge. This is contrary to rational choice theory, which predicts that dissidents' use of violence or its threat should force the state to make concessions to address their grievances. Instead, violence forces the public and government agents to focus on the threat terrorists pose and not their grievances.

Increased state repression drives all violent protesters, as well as those believed to be violent, underground into fugitive and clandestine trajectories,[61] which further narrows their worldview to an obsession about carrying out their violent mission at all costs to the exclusion of everything else. "Obsession" is the correct term here, for multiple failures, arrests, and deaths no longer deter them (again contrary to rational choice theory) from continuing to the bitter end. It is as if the violent goal takes control of these groups and their members' lives, thoughts, efforts, and emotions. This notion of obsession is consistent with new findings in social psychology. Having a definite goal in mind focuses attention selectively on relevant cues to that goal and filters out irrelevant ones. This "attentional blindness" has been demonstrated in laboratories and real life for individuals, though not groups. Nevertheless, it is easy to imagine that groups of individuals sharing a common focus may collectively fall prey to this cognitive mechanism in harmony, which makes it appear that their specific goal is in charge of their behavior. This condition challenges our intuition that our conscious executive self is in full control of these goal-oriented behaviors.[62]

The completion of the military goal turns off this obsessive drive. It has not been unusual in history for campaigns of political violence to end with perpetrators' spectacular violence.[63] A feeling of unfinished business seemed to motivate them to continue until they reach this dramatic ending, even in the absence of any political concessions, bringing about a sense of balance quenching their lust for further violence. Having attained this intermediary military goal, they could afford to pause and even step back to evaluate what they had done and see whether more violence furthered or hindered the achievement of their larger political goals.

The physical danger faced by both political challengers and state agents leads them to zealously support their respective comrades in their fight. This esprit de corps trumps any abstract political goals. At this stage, people fight more for their comrades than for their cause.[64] And combat suicide is the ultimate sacrifice for one's buddies and becomes the ultimate standard for heroism. The conflict becomes an end in itself, and violence then degenerates from politically motivated action into banditry.

This dynamic of violence leads to continuous campaigns of political violence. There are many temptations to escalate and very few to scale back, especially if political grievances persist; the state cannot eradicate the political protest community because it is too large; the violent protesters' active core survives; the state engages in indiscriminate repression of the protest community, with unfair, harsh punishment of its members; and the state prevents nonviolent protesters from returning to normal everyday life by declaring them outlaws—in essence making impermeable the boundaries between the protest community and society. All these measures put pressure on originally loose and informal politically violent protesters to organize into clandestine formal organizations with their own hierarchy, security, secrecy, and discipline and to narrow their social horizons in order to ensure their long-term survival.[65] Some bunches of violent guys consolidate or grow into a larger clandestine politically violent organization that can recruit or carry out operations from the top down, emulating formal military or intelligence organizations. This is seen in particular when they are supported by a larger organization or political party, of which they are just the military wing. Such support allows them to survive intense state repression. And so the cycle of violence and retaliation continues to escalate, with no end in sight. The final chapter examines potential approaches to break this cycle.

Chapter 5

Ending Political Violence in the West

As argued in the previous chapter, there are many temptations to escalate conflicts to campaigns of violence between political protesters and the state into cycles of intensifying retaliations on both sides but very few measures to scale them back. When faced with these political violence spirals, we naturally wonder how such campaigns ever end. Of the few studies on this issue, one reported that 10 percent of politically violent groups achieve victory, 43 percent adopt nonviolent tactics and join the political process, 40 percent are eradicated by the police, and 7 percent by the military.[1] Another study listed other endings: decapitation of leadership; failure by implosion, provoking a backlash or becoming marginalized; and transitioning to another type of violence such as banditry, insurgency, or war.[2]

These two surveys are insightful, but their shortcomings emerge if we use detailed historical descriptions of political violence outbreaks over a long time. Most political violence consists of one-time events easily repressed by the police, but sometimes the same political protest community may give rise to multiple campaigns of political violence with different results and temporary endings. For instance, the *sans-culottes* during the French Revolution were temporarily successful in helping the Montagne capture power during the Terror but ultimately were defeated by a reaction of police, national guards, army, and paramilitary units. However, this political protest community was not eradicated; it gave rise to the Babeuf conspiracy two years later. After effective repression under Napoleon, it reemerged again in Carbonari conspiracies during the 1820s and the successful 1830 insurrection. It suffered defeats in the 1832 and 1834 insurrections, and increasingly effective police repression shifted violence from mobs to small group attentats over the next decade. It reappeared, however, and again found success in the insurrection of February 1848 before the French army violently put it down four months later. It was resurrected in 1869 and especially in 1871 when the Commune ruled Paris for two months before the French army drowned it in blood and tried to eliminate it through deportation. Violence from this evolving community reemerged in the 1880s, culminating in the "era of the *attentats*" in the early 1890s, which was ended by police repression—but this time also fair trials (despite the notorious French Scoundrel Laws). There was a brief reemergence of violence with the tragic bandits twenty years later, which the police and army put down. This vague republican, liberal, and egalitarian political protest community, from *sans-culottes* to anarchists, lasted for more than 125 years until it joined the legal labor movement and was definitively eradicated by World War I.

A similarly prolonged and complicated trajectory characterized the half-century of democratic and liberal opposition to the tsar. Russian populists, repressed by the police, gave rise in 1879 to People's Will, which was eliminated by the state. Five years later, the Terrorist Faction of People's Will emerged briefly for one attentat. Finally, the Combat Unit of the Socialist Revolutionary Party emerged again 15 years later and self-destructed with the betrayal by its leader. However, its parent party survived to be part of the coalition that overthrew the tsarist regime in 1917, a victory made possible by the state's defeat in war.[3] The present global neojihad against the West has already lasted more than two decades and struck countries on both sides of the Atlantic.

I suspect that the two surveys mentioned would break up the long French and Russian campaigns of political violence into a dozen shorter ones with a dozen respective endings. However, these two campaigns of violence never fully ended: they were temporarily defeated only to reemerge again and again later. When basic grievances were not addressed, unfair police repression did not succeed in ending political violence, because it could not prevent new volunteers from restarting a new campaign a few years later. The French and Russian campaigns illustrate the same political protest community giving rise to multiple plots and attacks by unconnected bunches of violent guys, just like the homegrown attacks in the global neojihad in the West. The two surveys confined themselves to the small minority of campaigns of political violence conducted by one large single terrorist organization. Such violent organizations are rare though important, and they grow out of a bunch of violent guys. Such "bunches of guys" transform over time into hierarchical, disciplined, formal clandestine organizations.

Nevertheless, we should not dismiss the value of these two surveys; history provides plenty of instances of the endings they describe. These examples show that trying to end a campaign of violence by eradication or forceful repression is a very high-risk strategy and works only if the protest community is small enough. If it is too large to eradicate, it almost guarantees a sustained campaign of violence. A more effective ending of a campaign, not included in the above surveys, is the removal of grievances, such as the abolition of royal absolutism or the end of an unpopular war, like the Vietnam War, which eliminated support for the Weathermen in the United States in the 1970s.

Two other state strategies can be seen as applying the social identity perspective. The first is undermining the meaning of the challengers' social identity through betrayal by a prominent leader, which disillusions the rest of the violent in-group.[4] While betrayal by a common member just leads to anger against the traitor, reaffirming one's self-categorization, the betrayal by a prototype is perhaps too devastating for groups to survive.

The second campaign-ending strategy is to craft an overriding social identity whose salience trumps that of the in-group. This happens most frequently in nationalistic foreign wars, which force all members of a nation to rally around the state and suspend internal societal divisions for the duration of the war. This occurred in 1914 Europe where attacks by foreign nations trumped internal opposition to the capitalist-dominated state and many anarchists, socialists, and communists joined their respective national armies. Proximity to the danger was important to this rallying. In the United States, the threat of distant German armies was not strong enough to displace the salience of anarchist and socialist social identities for a nationalistic American one; there were many more war protesters from those groups in America than in Europe.

Most often, campaigns of political violence have ended through enlightened state strategy breaking the cycle of violence. This included focused and proportional repression against actual law breakers, in essence the isolation and fair removal of violent protesters from their parent community, a return to justice and fairness through impartial and transparent procedural justice with reasonable punishments, and procedures for addressing valid grievances in a legitimate way. Indeed, the social identity perspective argues that fair and respectful treatment of all societal members, especially impartiality to its minorities, is the defining characteristic of good national leadership for it fosters a common social identity, holds the country together, and encourages compliance with rules, commitment to the nation, and willingness of citizens to sacrifice for it.[5]

As we have seen, mutual escalation of conflict leads to the emergence and continuation of campaigns of violence. The key to containing and ending such campaigns is for the state to assess the threat accurately and not overreact. Accurate evaluation of the threat requires a good understanding of both nonviolent protesters and potentially violent ones. The state should not confuse the two, because this confusion leads it to unfairly punish legitimate and peaceful dissidents, often the first step to an escalation of violence. Unfortunately, Western states' indicators of "radicalization" in the present wave of global neojihad are really indicators of the generally nonviolent

Islamist protest community in the West,[6] and not its violent members. In fact, there is no objective or behavioral profile of political violent actors, except acts in furtherance around the outbreak of violence. However, there is a subjective profile—namely, a martial social identity indicating a willingness to use violence in defense of one's endangered community.

Distinguishing between peaceful and violent protesters may be difficult since the boundary between them is generally fluid and porous, not rigid and impermeable. Activists may go back and forth between the two categories, depending on the context, as violence in one context does not imply it in another. In general, violence is quite rare in the larger political community, which is generally hostile to it and its members who carry it out. The state should not prevent activists who have temporarily considered violence from going back to their peaceful activism. By declaring them outlaws and prosecuting such activists, by making the porous boundary between peaceful and violent protesters impermeable, the state needlessly turns temporary frustration and temptation into violence, as targeted activists are forced to go underground and turn to violence with fellow fugitives. Disproportionate punishment turns them into martyrs calling for revenge. This is especially true in the United States where conspiracy laws are so vague that they allow prosecution of people who have never been violent or committed any acts in furtherance. Instead, the state should try to bring such activists tempted by violence back into the fold by encouraging them to rejoin their peaceful colleagues. This requires creative skills but is the essence of good leadership.

If the state has probable cause to believe that segments of a political protest community are turning violent, its public protection mission demands that it should be able to monitor this threat. Intrusive surveillance violating citizens' civil rights and privacy should be sanctioned through due legal process by having impartial judges issue warrants for them. Systems in place throughout the West allow only law enforcement agencies to present evidence before such courts in a one-sided process in which state agents inevitably exaggerate their targets' threat,[7] leaving judges at the mercy of biased information. To counter this systemic bias, general public advocates with security clearance must be able to represent the interests of suspects without arousing suspicion among them. Good surveillance does not need to be limited to electronic monitoring of potential violent protesters but may also include infiltration of these networks.

Although the state has a legitimate interest in monitoring a political protest community when it has probable cause to believe that some members may turn violent, it is crucial that this monitoring be passive. State agents must be careful to be observers and not become agents provocateurs, influencing naïve protesters and creating crimes where none would have ever emerged. Entrapment is based on the myth of predisposition to political violence.[8] Such predisposition is very rare. Instead, the social identity perspective suggests that victims of entrapment model themselves on the agent provocateur, who presents himself or herself as the prototypical terrorist and a source of imitation for the victim.

Entrapment erodes a whole segment of society's trust in the state, for it views this tactic as a deceptive aggression against it, and in response, such measures activate politicized self-categorization in contrast to state agents. Within a political protest community, such tactics empower extremists claiming that the state is at war against their community. So far I have found no evidence that entrapment has prevented any real attack against society.[9] Without any clear benefit other than the bureaucratic imperative of bringing closure to ongoing investigations, such tactics foster distrust and disillusionment in the targeted community, increase the number of political protesters, and probably lead a few of them to engage in violence. Sting operations escalate state violence—it puts naïve wannabes in prison for a very long duration—without much benefit in terms of ending a campaign of violence, for its victims would probably not have participated in violence. Instead, the state must retain or regain protesters' trust and confidence that they can address their grievances within legitimate means; there is no role for deceptive practices like sting operations. The United States is alone in using them against political protesters for other Western countries rightfully condemn them as incompatible with liberal democracy.

When arresting or eliminating real threats, and especially when arresting entrapped protesters, the state must resist the temptation to indulge in gratuitous self-promotion. The media and politicians seldom pass up any opportunity to embellish and sensationalize news events and create an echo chamber fueling hysteria and panic in society over a rather negligible threat.[10] Elimination of a threat to national security can be accomplished without jingoistic flag waving. Self-generated frenzied alarmism not only escalates violence but also creates the environment for states to make drastic mistakes like the 2003 invasion of Iraq.

As we have seen, and contrary to alarmists' fears, the incidence of violence emerging from a political protest community is extremely small. This very low base rate of global neojihadi violence in the West makes talk of "the war on terror" particularly irresponsible. While extremist speech encourages the majority of the public to take this metaphor seriously and enthusiastically support its politicians especially during elections, such talk also leads it to acquiesce in the unjust and unfair treatment of Muslims in the West. This treatment alienates some Muslims who no longer feel part of the nation and may seek revenge for their perceived persecution not only against the state but more indiscriminately against society.

The present debate over national security versus civil rights is an oversimplification of the issues. There is no inherent contradiction between the two competing rights or permanent boundary dividing them. Any dividing line between them necessarily moves according to the context: in times of great danger, one must err toward national security; when the danger is past, civil rights must be reestablished. Citizens must always be on guard against their governments' tendency to make statements disproportionate to the real danger in order to artificially maintain a state of emergency for the sake of convenience in their protective mission. This leads to tyranny.

The United States is the most punitive Western nation, incarcerating about 1 percent of its population. Its strategy against potential violent protesters is likewise very punitive, in terms of both likelihood and duration of incarceration. An effective national leader tries to prevent protesters from crossing into violence, not with the threat of punishment, but by bringing them back to the national fold. The social identity perspective implies that threatening political protesters escalates a conflict and increases the probability of violence, while reintegrating them back into the national community defuses it. This second strategy, crafting a common sense of shared national identity, would prevent wannabes from crossing into violence—for one does not attack one's in-group. Crafting an inclusive sense of social identity is good leadership.

If the state is facing a foreign threat, its strategy must be proportional and focused retribution against specific perpetrators and containment of the threat. The state must not panic and conflate multiple local threats into a coordinated global one, like the mythical "anarchist international" of the late nineteenth century or seeing a communist conspiracy behind any domestic dissent in the middle of the twentieth century. Likewise, at present, many politicians, pundits, and ordinary people mistakenly believe that many local and independent insurgencies in the developing world are franchises of one gigantic al Qaeda or Daesh entity. To address these threats effectively, the state must deal with each in appropriate, measured, and targeted ways without missing real international connections between them.[11]

Most political violence is domestic. Here the state must calibrate measures to counter the threat according to the severity and imminence of the danger. When the threat is probable, the state may request an exceptional waver from usual policing practices from special courts to use more active measures to prevent the threat. These active measures may extend to temporary detention for prevention of a clear and imminent threat of mass casualties. To preserve civil rights, such measures must never be part of the normal policing repertoire and therefore be time limited, until the imminence of the threat is past. When danger of mass casualties reaches an emergent level, the state may apply an emergency provision for the exceptional use of deadly force to stop such an imminent threat. There must be fair, independent judicial oversight of these exceptional practices, including not only law enforcement representatives but also impartial judges and public advocates with security clearance. If state agents are wrong, they must be held accountable for their actions. Repressive measures must be proportional to the danger and focused on actual violent protesters, not their parent political community.

Once violent protesters are arrested, they should be subject to fair and transparent procedural justice with fair punishments. Judges overseeing these trials must be impartial, and viewed as such especially by the protest community. They should be particularly vigilant against prosecutorial misconduct, such as not turning over exonerating discovery material or making up inculpating evidence. Such prosecutorial or court malfeasance is unfortunately not a rarity in political cases, especially in the United States.[12] Prosecutors self-categorize as avengers of the victims of past crimes and may exceed the legal constraints of their job. Judges should be fair in ruling over pretrial motions and continue their impartiality in ruling over objections during trial. As humans and members of society, judges also self-categorize against societal protesters and routinely rule in favor of the prosecution— they must guard against such tendency. Sentences must be fair; I am skeptical about terrorist enhancement sentences in various Western countries. Political protesters rightly view them as unfair and discriminatory. After conviction, prisoners must be treated fairly. Their unfair treatment makes them martyrs and outrages their supporters, who then go on to become future perpetrators. Fair punishment of actual perpetrators does not elicit moral outrage.

In the turn to political violence, identity trumps both ideology and self-interest. Once the state understands this perspective, it will know how to prevent and fight political violence. The formula boils down to good state leadership in the treatment of its multiple constituencies, especially its visible minorities, to prevent alienation of one of them and thus its activation into a political protest community, vigilance not to escalate hostilities with such a community, and the fair, focused, and proportional repression of violent protesters. This will prevent the emergence of a campaign of political violence, undermine it if prevention fails, and more important, realize the hope of a true liberal democracy.

This hope may run against nature. The social identity perspective suggests that political violence is the natural result of evolutionary cognitive mechanisms that make us identify and favor our group at the expense of strangers. The challenge for the prevention of political violence is to transcend our nature at the very moment when it is most difficult to do so: when escalation of conflict, with its verbal belligerence, disillusionment with peaceful solutions, and outrage at out-group aggression, push us to retaliate with violence. Those most caring and self-sacrificing for their group, because they identify most with it, are most at peril to turn to violence.

Transcending our human nature will remain a constant and difficult challenge but one necessary for human survival. Political violence originates in self-categorization, which helped small groups survive in hostile environments during our evolution. Now self-categorization has the potential to lead to annihilation, as we have developed weapons capable of wiping out the human race. The last century's world wars have sadly demonstrated our willingness to use them for nationalism—a self-categorization. Although violence may have dramatically decreased over the past seven centuries in the West due to the better angels of our nature,[13] survival now requires eternal vigilance against the demons of our nature to guard ourselves against vicious cycles of political violence.

Notes

Introduction

1 Despite the fact that any Google search of my name will iden-tify this agency because my employment had been leaked by a senate committee, it recently sent me a letter reminded me "that the official status [classified] of your past association with the organization has not changed." Henceforth, I shall refrain from confirming or deny-ing anything about my association with that agency.

2 Rick McCauley, Ian Lustick, Paul Roazen, Brendan O'Leary, Marc Ross, John Sabini, Bob Vitalis, Art Waldron, Rob deRubeis, Randall Collins, and Doug Massey, among others, were frequent participants in the SACSEC seminars. Some of their later publica-tions in terrorism research include Clark McCauley and Sophia Moskalenko, 2011; Marianne Heiberg, Brendan O'Leary, and John Tirman, 2007; and Ian Lustick, 2006.

3 Christopher Browning, 1992.

4 Daniel Goldhagen, 1996.

5 This group is often referred to ISIL, ISIS (Islamic State in Iraq and Syria), or Daesh (after the Arabic initials of the group). I use Daesh, as it is the most accurate of the acronyms.

6 See Sageman, 2004, and Fawaz Gerges, 2005.

7 Especially Jocelyne Cesari, 1997; Mohammed Hafez, 2003; Gilles Kepel, 1991, 1993, 1994, and 2002; Farhad Khosrokhavar, 1997 and 2002; Olivier Roy, 1994; Jenny White, 2002; Carrie Wickham, 2002; and Quintan Wiktorowicz, 2001.

8 See Elihu Katz and Paul Lazarsfeld, 1964 and the special 50th anniversary volume dedicated to this work in Peter Simonson, ed., 2006.

9 Rodney Stark, 1997.

10 Stark and Bainbridge, 1980, 1985, and 1996; Bainbridge, 1997; and Stark and Finke, 2000. This led me to the empirical research on cult recruitment in Eileen Barker, 1986; Marc Galanter, 1990; and Johan Lofland, 1981.

11 Especially Mark Granovetter, 1973, 1983, and 1985.

12 Sageman, 2004.

13 Sageman, 2004: 144–45.

14 Some of this work is summarized in Atran, 2010.

15 Sageman, 2010. I thank the local researchers, social workers, journalists, and law enforcement officers who guided me through these neighborhoods and introduced me to people to interview. The resulting study has still not been released by the Air Force.

16 Sageman, 2008. I submitted that book to my former employer for review since I had gathered my information from contemporaneous classified data but had been careful not to be specific enough to betray any secret. The book was returned without a single change.

17 Sageman, 2008: 125–46.

18 Bruce Hoffman, 2008. I believed that the review was so ridiculous that it did not deserve a reply, but most colleagues in the intelligence community urged me to respond. However, the editors of the journal prevented me from addressing these outrageous distortions by limiting me to a few hundred words.

19 Our continuous conversations about what we saw resulted in Mitchell Silber, 2012, which showed that, even in al Qaeda operations abroad, the al Qaeda factor varied greatly from tight command and control to just providing inspiration to unconnected global neojihadi terrorists.

20 Sebastian Rotella comes to mind. His series of articles on David Coleman Headley are unequaled in their accuracy and depth because they are based on several years of intense research, when he traveled to Europe, Morocco, India, and of course the United States in pursuit of the target.

21 They do not have access to discovery material in terrorism cases, which is much richer than anything in their database because

it consists of raw information, not just FBI reports of conversations tailored to further prosecution.

Chapter 1

1 Global neojihadi organizations are violently anti-Shi'a, which excludes Hezbollah, a Shi'a organization that has projected violence into the West. It makes no sense to lump Hezbollah attacks with al Qaeda attacks, as they are sworn enemies and represent very different dynamics and strategies.

2 Brian Neal Vinas was a member of al Qaeda who always refused to attack the West, despite erroneous reporting by Paul Cruickshank, Nic Robertson, and Ken Shiffman, 2010. See his testimony in *U.S. v. Medunjanin*, April 23, 2012: 1139–42. He never pled guilty to any charges related to killing Americans at home; see *U.S. v. John Doe [Brian Neal Vinas]*, January 28, 2009.

3 I am referring to Khalid Sheikh Mohammed's confession during his Combatant Status Review Tribunal Hearing; see U.S. Department of Defense, 2007b. There were no acts in furtherance of the vast majority of these plans.

4 Trevor Aaronson, 2013, shows that these critics are not far off the mark.

5 Jenkins, 2010: 10.

6 I was the defense's expert witness at his 1995 trial. Harris was clearly suffering from schizophrenia and died in prison months after his conviction from a ruptured brain aneurysm.

7 I was a consultant for the defense and reviewed his extensive psychiatric history of bipolar affective disorder. See *State of Washington v. Naveed Haq*, 2009. Without any link to international terrorism, he was tried in state rather than federal court and convicted of aggravated murder and a hate crime.

8 This might not be true in the United States, as most defendants take a plea and the evidence does not become public record.

9 Eliane Barbieri and Jytte Klausen, 2012; Peter Bergen and Bruce Hoffman, 2010; Jerome Bjelopera and Mark Randol, 2010; James Carafano, Steve Bucci, and Jessica Zuckerman, 2012; Brian Jenkins, 2010; Javier Jordan, 2012; Jytte Klausen, 2010; John Mueller

and Mark Stewart, 2015; Petter Nesser, 2008 and 2010; Sageman, 2009; Robin Simcox and Emily Dyer, 2013; Robin Simcox, Hannah Stuart, and Houriya Ahmed, 2010; Jeffrey Thomas, 2011.

10 Bergen and Hoffman, 2010: 5.

11 Jenkins, 2010: 6, 8.

12 Bergen and Hoffman, 2010, argued this point by focusing exclusively on this third peak.

13 Jenkins, 2010: 13.

14 See Silber, 2012.

15 See *R. v. Khyam et al.*, 2006–2007.

16 I have excluded the Madrid bombings and discuss my reasons for doing so later in this chapter.

17 For instance, Ali Saleh al Marri, Zacarias Moussaoui, Jose Padilla, Iyman Faris, Christian Ganczarski, Karim Mehdi, Rangzieb Ahmed, Aleem Nasir, Maqsood Lodin, or Yusuf Ocak, among others.

18 See National Commission on Terrorist Attacks upon the United States, 2004; Bergen, 2006; Steve Coll, 2004; Terry McDermott, 2005; and Lawrence Wright, 2006.

19 *MP c/ Daoudi, Beghal, Bounour et al.*, 2005; Cour d'appel de Bruxelles, 2004; see also Jean-Louis Bruguière, 2009: 422–34.

20 See Saajid Badat's extensive testimonies in US courts, *U.S. v. Medunjanin*, March 29, 2012; *U.S. v. Mustafa*, April 28 and 29, 2014; *U.S. v. abu Gaith*, March 10 and 11, 2014.

21 *R. v. Khyam et al.*, 2006–2007; *R. v. Khawaja*, 2005; *R. v. Khawaja*, 2008.

22 See Lindsay Clutterbuck, 2014; Raffaelo Pantucci, 2015: 176–83; Silber, 2012: 68–82; *Dhiren Barot and R.*, 2007; Senate Select Committee on Intelligence, 2012: 258–76.

23 *Dhiren Barot and R.*, 2007: paragraphs 25, 27, and 29.

24 Senate Select Committee on Intelligence, 2012: 275.

25 Pantucci, 2012; Robertson, Cruickshank, and Lister, 2012a, 2012b.

26 *R. v. Shakil et al.*, 2008; *R. v. Shakil et al.*, 2009.

27 *R. v. Ibrahim et al.*, 2007.

28 *R. v. Ali et al.*, 2008.

29 See Michael Taarnby, 2014.

30 Pantucci, 2010.

31 See Special Immigration Appeals Commission, 2010.

32 *U.S. v. Medunjanin*, 2012.

33 Peter Nesser and Brynjar Lia, 2010.

34 David Coleman Headley, in *U.S. v. Rana*, 2011: 56–1189.

35 Ray Weaver, 2012a.

36 Weaver, 2012b. One of the leaders of the conspiracy who testified in his defense claimed they had come to Copenhagen because his coconspirator wanted a Big Mac from McDonald's.

37 Annette Ramelsberger, 2012.

38 Subtracting the six Hamburg conspirators from the total of 23 since they were radicalized in the West.

39 See *MP c/ Brigitte et Mir*, 2007, for the French side of the investigation, and *R. v. Lodhi*, 2006, for the Australian side of the investigation.

40 Guido Steinberg, 2013: 59–76.

41 Fernando Reinares, 2014b. Eleven were convicted at the trial, but the Spanish Supreme court later acquitted six of them.

42 *U.S. v. Shahzad*, 2010.

43 See Lorenzo Vidino, 2014: 35.

44 See John Chilcot et al., 2016.

45 See Bart Schuurman, Quirine Eijkman, and Edwin Bakker, 2015, and Janny Groen and Annieke Kranenberg, 2010.

46 *R. v. Benbrika and Ors*, 2011, and *R. (C'Wealth) v. Elomar and Ors*, 2010.

47 Reinares, 2014a. The discovery material included the 1,471-page indictment (Juzgado Central de Instruccion No. 6, 2006), about half of which was a laborious listing of all the telephone calls all the Madrid suspects made. There was no trace of any call or text from Pakistan, unlike real al Qaeda linked cases, where such communications have been found. Reinares cites "senior intelligence officers of Western states" for his sources (Reinares, 2014a: endnotes, 55, 60, 81, and 99). However, he had made the same claims in Reinares, 2010, before he ever met his alleged sources and has ignored other intelligence sources who contradicted his claims. Reinares claimed that this link to al Qaeda was Amer Azizi, who allegedly came to Spain at the end of 2003. However, there is no evidence of this alleged trip and the evolution of the attack can be carefully traced without requiring his presence. The al Qaeda leaders, who Reinares cited as working with Azizi (Reinares, 2014a: 43–44—namely, Abdal Hadi al Iraqi and Abu Faraj al Libi), have been captured and extensively debriefed, but there is no mention in them of

Azizi or the Madrid bombings. See US Department of Defense, 2007a, 2007c, and 2008; and *U.S. v. Abdal Hadi al Iraqi*, 2014.

48 See also Scott Atran, 2010: 168–224, my collaborator in this search. Having intensively reviewed all the classified documents on this issue because of this controversy, I am extremely skeptical of Reinares's claim.

49 *R. v. Fattal and Ors*, 2011.

50 Nesser, 2012.

51 Jenkins, 2011, suggested the use of "stray dog," implying wandering away from a pack.

52 Undetected: incidents 4, 6, 7, 9, 12, 14, 16, 21, 31, 37, 42, 46, 50, 52, 54, 56, 58, 60, and 63. Causing serious injury: incidents 12, 14, 21, 46, 52, 56, and 63.

53 Hoffman, 2008.

54 Hoffman and Reinares, eds., 2014.

55 Hoffman and Reinares, eds., 2014: xii.

56 Javier Jordan, 2014, relied on very questionable Moroccan press reporting for his description of an alleged plot in Italy. The alleged plotters never set foot in Italy and hoped to rely on relatives living in Italy, who were unaware of the plot. Vidino, 2014, in his summary of jihadism in Italy does not even mention this incident. The other alleged plot was the French Ansar al-Fatah network of neojihadi militants, who talked much but did nothing. They were convicted only of forming an association whose goal was to prepare a terrorist act. See *MP c/ Melliti, Bouhalli, Ferchichi et autres*, 2008. There were no acts in furtherance in either case, therefore not meeting inclusion criteria in my survey.

57 Incidents 14, 15, 18 (17, 21, 23, and 27 collapsed into one case), 25, 29, 30, 32, 38, 39, and 40.

Chapter 2

1 Jenkins, 1977: 8.

2 See Cherif Bassiouni, ed., 1975; Barton Ingraham, 1979; Otto Kirchheimer, 1961; Nicholas Kittrie and Eldon Wedlock, eds., 1998; and Geoffrey Stone, 2004.

3 By the West, I include Australia, New Zealand, the United States, Canada, and the Western European countries.

4 Jenkins, 2010: 13.

5 See the Nobel Prize–winning work done by Daniel Kahneman and Amos Tversky. See Daniel Kahneman, Paul Slovic, and Amos Tversky, eds., 1982; Kahneman and Tversky, 2000; Thomas Gilovich, Dale Griffin, and Daniel Kahneman, 2002. See also Kahneman's 2011 best seller.

6 Kahneman, Slovic, and Tversky, eds., 1982: 157.

7 NCTC, 2013: 51. This 166-page manual for the inclusion of individuals on various watchlists was approved on March 12, 2013, by the deputies of all US departments involved in national security.

8 Transportation Security Intelligence Service, 2002: slide 3.

9 Clayton Grigg, 2015: 2–3; Bart Elias, William Krouse, and Ed Rappaport, 2005: 1–3.

10 NCTC, 2013: 51.

11 *Rebecca Gordon et al. v. FBI et al.*, 2003, for instance.

12 NCTC, 2013: 51.

13 NCTC, 2013: 51–52.

14 NCTC, 2013: 35; italics added for emphasis.

15 NCTC, 2013: 43.

16 NCTC, 2013: 38–42; italics added for emphasis. This watering down of criteria for inclusion into a terrorist watchlist recalls the Security Index, the FBI's notorious and illegal list of 26,000 alleged "subversives" to be arrested and put in concentration camps at the start of any national emergency. When the Security Index was specifically outlawed in 1971, it was renamed the Administrative Index and illegally continued to exist until at least 1978. See Betty Medsger, 2014: 248–65. In fact, the Patriot Act reinstates many of the features of the FBI's outlawed COINTELPRO program.

17 NCTC, 2013: 10–11.

18 Michael Steinbach, 2015: 7; NCTC, 2013: 19.

19 NCTC, 2013: 33. These words are lifted verbatim from the 1968 US Supreme Court decision in *Terry v. Ohio*, 392 U.S. 1, and were later adopted in the 1970s in directives aimed at curbing previous illegal FBI activities.

20 NCTC, 2013: 34.

21 NCTC, 2013: 35.

22 NCTC, 2013: 52–53.

23 NCTC, 2013: 21.

24 Grigg, 2015: 6.

25 Steinbach, 2015: 12.

26 Alex Schmid, 1984: 76.

27 This is the opposite of the scientific process, which tries to prove a hypothesis wrong and, failing that, temporarily adopts it as true.

28 Directorate of Terrorist Identities, 2013: 2.

29 National Security Division, 2012.

30 John Mueller and Mark Stewart, 2015: 138, provide a base rate of 3 per 100 million per year chance of being killed in a terrorist act in the United States from 2002 to 2013. I look at the number of terrorists, not the number killed, but the two very low base rates are in the same ballpark.

31 Steinbach, 2015: 4.

32 I scored Babar as attending a camp for two days but not getting any training there, since he was really accompanying others to the camp. Boyd attended a camp almost 20 years before he was arrested when he resurrected his interest in jihad.

33 Bledsoe's attack seemed spontaneous as a target of opportunity presented itself to him, and therefore he did not indicate prior intent. Hasan's attack was of course very deliberate but extremely secretive, without any prior indication of intent detected.

34 See Jeremy Scahill and Ryan Devereaux, 2014.

35 NCTC, 2013: 38–42.

36 *U.S. v. Mohamud*, 2013, and personal interview, May 17 and 18, 2012.

37 NCTC, 2013: 54.

38 Grigg, 2015: 6; Steinbach, 2015: 6; and Piehota, 2014.

39 I cannot comment on the effectiveness of the watchlists in keeping these foreigners out because of lack of empirical data to conduct a Bayesian analysis, but I suspect that they have been much less effective than the government claims.

Chapter 3

1 Sageman, 2014.

2 Schmid, 1984: 76.

3 See Sageman, 2017, for an elaboration of this definition.

4 Kahneman, 2011. The set of associations with a term like terrorist comes easily and naturally to mind and are part of what Kahneman calls system 1, subject to all kinds of cognitive biases and heuristics. The ability to logically analyze this term calls for much greater cognitive effort and energy, part of what he calls system 2.

5 See Lee Ross and Richard Nisbett, 1991: 119–44.

6 See Maxwell Taylor, 1988; Walter Reich, ed., 1990; Martha Crenshaw, ed., 1995; Andrew Silke, ed., 2003; John Horgan, 2005: 47–106; and Sageman, 2004: 83–91, for a summary and critique of the terrorist personality approach. Nevertheless, mental health professionals, who have never examined a terrorist, and amateur psychologists persist in believing that terrorists suffer from some sort of mental disorder on the basis of very selective secondhand anecdotal evidence. Adam Lankford, 2013, is just one of the latest examples.

7 Jerrold Post, 2007: 37.

8 Post, 2007: 101–58.

9 Ariel Merari, 2010: 142–45.

10 According to the official definition in American Psychiatric Association, 2013: 647. Merari based his finding on his lay understanding of mental disorder and on the use of the controversial Rorschach inkblot test, whose validity is increasingly questioned.

11 See Arie Kruglanski, Xiaoyan Chen, Mark Dechesne, Shira Fishman, and Edward Orehek, 2009.

12 Albert Borowitz, 2005.

13 Quintan Wiktorowicz, 2005: 85–98.

14 See, for instance, Sageman, 2008: 3–11, 52–57. Viewing the atrocities in Bosnia and the killing of a Palestinian boy caused the respective future terrorists to experience intense moral outrage that changed their perspective of the world and motivated them to do something about it. The next chapter describes this mechanism.

15 Enyo, 2009, and Mary Habeck, 2006, are examples of such literature. This ideological argument has been soundly refuted by a consensus of true scholars of political Islam. See Khaled Abou el Fadl, 2005; Raymond Baker, 2003; Richard Bonney, 2004; François Burgat, 2005; Jocelyne Cesari, 2004; Michael Cooke, 2000; Patricia Crone, 2004; John Esposito, 1999 and 2002; Fawaz Gerges, 2005; Mohammed Hafez, 2003; Gilles Kepel, 2002 and 2004; Farhad

Notes to Pages 96–107.

Khosrokhavar, 1997 and 2002; Olivier Roy, 2004; Carrie Wickham, 2002; and Wiktorowicz, ed., 2004. However, for the true believers in the ideological thesis, the academic refusal to "blame it on Islam" is rejected as political correctness.

16 This is the premise of many "counter-radicalization" programs such as the Quilliam Foundation in Britain or the Centre de Prévention contre les Dérives Sectaires liées à l'Islam in France.

17 Eric Hoffer, 1963.

18 Gustave Le Bon, 1895/1998.

19 Post, 2007: 193. Apparently, Post seems to believe that this subordination of an individual to the group is a pathological process. As we will later see, this is actually a common, normal, and natural phenomenon.

20 See Mia Bloom, 2005; Diego Gambetta, ed., 2005; Mohammed Hafez, 2007; Merari, 2010; Robert Pape, 2005; and Ami Pedahzur, 2005.

21 This is the view promoted by Rohan Gunaratna, 2002, but see also Post, 2007: 204–5. This was also the view from law enforcement; see Mitchell Silber and Arvin Bhatt, 2007.

22 See Aaronson, 2013.

23 George Michael, 2012; Petter Nesser, 2012; Raffaello Pantucci, 2011; and Jeffrey Simon, 2013.

24 See Ronald Clarke and Greame Newman, 2006.

25 Simon Perry and Badi Hasisi, 2015.

26 See Amir Rosenmann, Gerhard Reese, and James Cameron, 2016.

27 Alexis de Tocqueville, 1986: 761–62.

28 These terms are used by Marxists, social movement theorists, social psychologists, and Max Taylor, respectively.

29 This is the concept of availability heuristics. See Kahneman, Slovic, and Tversky, eds., 1982: 163–208, and Kahneman, 2011: 129–45.

30 Ted Gurr, 1970.

31 For instance, the 1970s Weathermen, Baader-Meinhof gang, and Italian Red Brigades. Some members of the current wave of global neojihadi terrorists are also children of the elite of their respective countries.

32 John McCarthy and Mayer Zald, 1977.

33 See Doug McAdam, Sidney Tarrow, and Charles Tilly, 2001. This focus on social mechanism is mostly the work of Charles Tilly.

34 McAdam, 1982.

35 McAdam, 1986 and 1988.

36 See previous chapter. At a recent conference, a government contractor claimed to have constructed a reliable screening tool on the basis of these alleged signature behaviors. However, when questioned, the presenter did not understand the basic notions of sensitivity and specificity required to test the accuracy of these instruments.

Chapter 4

1 Solomon Asch, 1956.

2 Stanley Milgram, 1974.

3 Philip Zimbardo, 2007.

4 Lee Ross and Richard Nisbett, 1991.

5 See Randy Borum, 2004, a non-peer-reviewed pamphlet; Fathali Moghaddam, 2005 and 2006; and Michael King and Donald Taylor's 2011 critical review of their models.

6 Clark McCauley and Sophia Moskalenko, 2011; McCauley, 2008: 2–3; and Isabelle Sommier, 2008.

7 Andy Martens, Raazesh Sainudiin, Chris Sibley, Jeff Schimel, and David Webber, 2014, for empirical evidence for violence as escalation of conflict.

8 McCauley and Moskalenko, 2011: 214.

9 Jacquelien van Stekelenburg and Bert Klandermans, 2007; and van Stekelenburg, 2013 and 2014.

10 See Sommier, 2008, or Jacques Semelin, 2007, for examples of these theories. This concept of social identity is also a more accurate description of what Daniela Pisoiu, 2012, conceptualizes as an occupation in her insightful book.

11 Other well-known social scientific attempts to understand how the Holocaust was possible include studies about authoritarian personality (Adorno, Frenkel-Brunswik, Levinson, and Sanford, 1950), the nature of prejudice (Allport, 1954), obedience (Milgram, 1974), and the power of the situation (Zimbardo, 2007), which in turn influenced historical explanations of the Holocaust (Browning, 1992).

12 See John Turner, 1996; Haslam, Reicher, and Reynolds, 2012; and Matthew Hornsey, 2008.

13 It is probably part of what cognitive psychologists call system 1; see Kahneman, 2011: 19–105.

14 Turner, 1991: 155–73.

15 For instance, see Bill Buford's 1993 description of his gradual and insidious depersonalization within a group of soccer fans, which led him to participate in crowd violence. He became a soccer hooligan without realizing it.

16 Michael Hogg and Scott Reid, 2006.

17 Albert Bandura, 1990.

18 Stephen Reicher, Nick Hopkins, Mark Levine, and Rakshi Rath, 2005: 624–25.

19 See Penelope Oakes, Alexander Haslam, and John Turner, 1994, for further analysis on the relationship between social categories and social reality.

20 Oakes, Haslam, and Turner, 1994: 116–24.

21 Oakes, Haslam, and Turner, 1994: 96.

22 This is Kahneman and Tversky's availability heuristic.

23 This is basically Benedict Anderson's 1991 argument adapted to political communities instead of nations.

24 See George Lakoff, 1987. See also Kahneman, Slovic, and Tversky, eds., 1982: 23–98, and Gilovich, Griffin, and Kahneman, 2002: 49–81, for some of the common cognitive biases deriving from this type of automatic thinking.

25 Alexander Haslam, Stephen Reicher, and Michael Platow, 2011: 64–73. This sort of vagueness need not be an impediment to rigorous social science analysis as shown by Charles Ragin, 2000.

26 Haslam, Reicher, and Platow, 2011: 55–64.

27 Turner, Oakes, Haslam, and McGarty, 1994.

28 Reicher, Hopkins, Levine, and Rath, 2005; Haslam, Reicher, and Platow, 2011: 165–95.

29 This is Borowitz's 2005 previously mentioned Herostratos Syndrome. This single factor should not be stretched too much to explain the full complexity of violent political behavior.

30 See Mancur Olson, 1971; Haslam, Reicher, and Platow, 2011: 109–35.

31 See José Marques, Dominic Abrams, Dario Páez, and Michael Hogg, 2003, for a review of this literature. We shall see this same phenomenon within each rebel group, as they seek to punish their own betrayers or police spies. This is not always the case in liberal democracies as shown in Ingraham, 1979, but this depends on whether the rebel is viewed as legitimate or not at the time.

32 Sageman, 2004: 107–12.

33 Donatella della Porta, 2013: 70–112, and McCauley and Moskalenko, 2011: 154–60, come to mind.

34 See Haslam, Reicher, and Platow, 2011: 85–87, for an elegant mathematical demonstration of this dynamic.

35 Alexander Haslam, Penelope Oakes, Craig McGarty, John Turner, and Rina Onorato, 1995.

36 I wish to thank Alex Haslam and Steve Reicher for suggesting this general line of reasoning in private communications on July 9 and 22, 2013, respectively.

37 Patrice Gueniffey, 2000: 125, 230, makes a similar argument for the violence of the French Revolution.

38 Reicher and Haslam, 2006; Haslam and Reicher, 2007.

39 Olson, 1971.

40 Albert Hirschman, 1970.

41 This escalation in the intensity of activities or increased proselytism is often seen in the cognitive dissonance literature. See Leon Festinger, Henry Riecken, and Stanley Schachter, 1964. I'm not sure why Hirschman did not include this doubling down of effort to redress a declining group in his possible alternatives.

42 See Jeff Goodwin, James Jasper, and Francesca Polletta, eds., 2001.

43 It is clear that from in-group reactions to martyrs, what global neojihadis call martyrs are really heroes to them, not martyrs. The English translation of the Arabic *shahid* means a witness (for God). Traditionally, a *shahid* is a warrior who dies in battle for the sake of God. Such a dead warrior would be a hero and not a martyr in the sense developed here because his death was fair.

44 This action can be an escalation of peaceful protest in the case of martyrs for nonviolence: Jesus, Gandhi, and Martin Luther King Jr.

45 José Marques, Vincent Yzerbyt, and Jacques-Philippe Leyens, 1988; and Marques, Abrams, Páez, and Hogg, 2003.

46 See Nisbett and Cohen, 1996.

47 Despite the lack of self-awareness, this model can still be tested in the laboratory in the way people process imagined action against respective in-group or out-group members. See the experiments in moral reasoning by Joshua Greene, 2013, and Jonathan Haidt, 2012, which are predicated on potential victims being members of one's in-group. I suspect that their robust experimental results might be reversed if victims were members of an out-group.

48 Albert Camus, 1977: 571–79 (in *L'Homme Révolté*).

49 See Greene, 2013, and Haidt, 2012, for popular summaries of this new field.

50 Henri Tajfel, 1970; Tajfel, 1982; Tajfel and Turner, 1979; See also Russell Spears and Sabine Otten, 2012.

51 Frantz Fanon, 1961, described this phenomenon in a colonial community.

52 Olson, 1971.

53 Della Porta, 2013: 252–60, has also observed this same phenomenon, which she calls "cognitive closure."

54 This type of thinking is also popularly referred to as "black and white" or dichotomous thinking. See Post, 2007: 15–37 for an example of such a reductionist analysis of "hatred bred into the bone."

55 This of course holds only when the state and government is representative of society. In cases of a minority having power, like colonial countries, the majority population may support these self-categorized soldiers and bring about liberation from this ruling minority.

56 Sageman, 2017.

57 See Mia Bloom, 2005, for an example of how militant group competition facilitates political violence.

58 See Kenneth Keniston, 1968: 47.

59 I elaborate on this process in a forthcoming book on global neojihadi attacks in London.

60 Vera Figner, 1991: 116.

61 See Della Porta, 2013, for an analysis of clandestine political violence.

62 See John Bargh, Peter Gollwitzer, and Gabriele Oettingen, 2010: 288–306, for a review of this intriguing literature.

63 For instance, People's Will's assassination of Tsar Alexander II, Fenian Skirmishers' twin bombings of the Tower of London and Parliament, Sante Caserio's assassination of French President Carnot, and Mario Buda's Wall Street bombing.

64 This is similar to the findings in World War II that American troops fought more for their buddies than for ideology; see Samuel Stouffer et al., 1965: 105–91.

65 The gradual transformations of Land and Liberty into People's Will in 1870s Russia and more recently SDS into Weathermen are good examples of this process.

Chapter 5

1 Seth Jones and Martin Libicki, 2008: 18–20.

2 Audrey Cronin, 2009.

3 Sageman, 2017, provides a detailed description of these two large campaigns of political violence.

4 The Russian Socialist Revolutionary Party's Combat Unit never recovered from the betrayal of its chief Avno Azef (Sageman, 2017), and the British infiltration of the Fenian Skirmishers' leadership in the 1880s undermined this group; see Niall Whelehan, 2012, and Joseph McKenna, 2012.

5 Haslam, Reicher, and Platow, 2011: 109–20.

6 For instance, some of the indicators on the British Prevent Program, or on the new French government indicators at http://www.stop-djihadisme.gouv.fr/decrypter.html.

7 Sageman, 2014: 573–74, explains this alarmist tendency within state agencies.

8 Federal law on entrapment requires proof of a predisposition to violence for conviction.

9 See also Aaronson, 2013, and Ian Lustick, 2006, for an analysis of these tactics in the present global neojihadi wave of terrorism.

10 Lustick, 2006; Mueller, 2006; Mueller and Stewart, 2015; and chapter 2.

11 The failure to understanding the international dimension of the first World Trade Center bombing in 1993 unnecessarily delayed combating the global neojihadi threat against the United States.

12 See the Haymarket bombing trial, the Homestead attentat trial, and the Mooney-Billings and Sacco and Vanzetti frame-ups, continuing to the 1960s trials against New Left militants and more recent trials against Muslims.

13 Steven Pinker, 2011.

References

Aaronson, Trevor. 2013. *The Terror Factory: Inside the FBI's Manufactured War on Terrorism*. Brooklyn: Ig Publishing.

Abou el Fadl, Khaled. 2005. *The Great Theft: Wrestling Islam from the Extremists*. New York: HarperCollins.

Adorno, T. W., Frenkel-Brunswik, Else, Levinson, Daniel, and Sanford, Nevitt. 1950. *The Authoritarian Personality*. New York: Harper and Brothers.

Alimi, Eitan, Demetriou, Chares, and Bosi, Lorenzo. 2015. *The Dynamics of Radicalization: A Relational and Comparative Perspective*. New York: Oxford University Press.

Allport, Gordon. 1954. *The Nature of Prejudice*. Cambridge, MA: Addison-Wesley.

American Psychiatric Association. 2013. *Diagnostic and Statistical Manual of Mental Disorders, Fifth Edition*. Washington, DC: American Psychiatric Publishing.

Anderson, Benedict. 1991. *Imagined Communities: Reflections on the Origin and Spread of Nationalism*, rev. ed. London: Verso.

Asch, Solomon. 1956. "Studies of Independence and Conformity: A Minority of One against a Unanimous Majority." *Psychological Monographs: General and Applied* 70, no. 9: 1–70.

Atran, Scott. 2010. *Talking to the Enemy: Faith, Brotherhood, and the (Un)making of Terrorists*. New York: HarperCollins.

References

Bainbridge, William. 1997. *The Sociology of Religious Movements*. New York: Routledge.

Baker, Raymond. 2003. *Islam without Fear: Egypt and the New Islamists*. Cambridge, MA: Harvard University Press.

Bandura, Albert. 1990. "Mechanisms of Moral Disengagement." In Reich, 161–91.

Barbieri, Eliane Tschaen, and Klausen, Jytte. 2012. "Al Qaeda's London Branch: Patterns of Domestic and Transnational Network Integration." *Studies in Conflict and Terrorism* 35: 411–31.

Bargh, John, Gollwitzer, Peter, and Oettingen, Gabriele. 2010. "Motivation." In *Handbook of Social Psychology, Fifth Edition*, edited by Susan Fiske, Daniel Gilbert, and Gardner Lindzey, 268–316. Hoboken, NJ: John Wiley and Sons.

Barker, Eileen. 1986. *The Making of a Moonie: Choice or Brainwashing?* Oxford: Basil Blackwell.

Bassiouni, Cherif, ed. 1975. *International Terrorism and Political Crimes*. Springfield, IL: Charles C. Thomas.

Bergen, Peter. 2006. *The Osama bin Laden I Know: An Oral History of al Qaeda's Leader*. New York: Free Press.

———. 2016. *United States of Jihad: Investigating America's Homegrown Terrorists*. New York: Crown.

Bergen, Peter, and Hoffman, Bruce. 2010, September 10. "Assessing the Terrorist Threat: A Report of the Bipartisan Policy Center's National Security Preparedness Group." Washington, DC: Bipartisan Policy Center. Available at http://bipartisanpolicy.org/library/report/assessing -terrorist-threat.

Bjelopera, Jerome, and Randol, Mark. 2010, September 20. "American Jihadist Terrorism: Combating a Complex Threat." Washington, DC: Congressional Research Service. Available at http://www.fas.org/sgp/crs/terror/R41416.pdf.

Bloom, Mia. 2005. *Dying to Kill: The Allure of Suicide Terror*. New York: Columbia University Press.

Bonney, Richard. 2004. *Jihad: From Qur'an to bin Laden*. Houndmills, Hampshire: Palgrave Macmillan.

References

Borowitz, Albert. 2005. *Terrorism for Self-Glorification: The Herostratos Syndrome*. Kent, OH: Kent State University Press.

Borum, Randy. 2004. *Psychology of Terrorism*. Tampa: University of South Florida.

Browning, Christopher. 1992. *Ordinary Men: Reserve Police Battalion 101 and the Final Solution in Poland*. New York: HarperCollins.

Bruguière, Jean-Louis. 2009. *Ce que je n'ai pas pu dire: Entretiens avec Jean-Marie Pontaut*. Paris: Éditions Robert Laffont.

Buford, Bill. 1993. *Among the Thugs*. New York: Vintage.

Burgat, François. 2005. *L'islamisme à l'heure d'Al-Qaida*. Paris: Éditions La Découverte.

Camus, Albert. 1977. *Essais*. Paris: Bibliothèque de la Pléiade, NRF, Éditions Gallimard.

Carafano, James, Bucci, Steve, and Zuckerman, Jessica. 2012, April 25. "Fifty Terror Plots Foiled since 9/11: The Homegrown Threat and the Long War on Terrorism." *The Heritage Foundation Backgrounder*, no. 2682. Available at http://thf_media.s3.amazonaws.com/2012/pdf/bg2682 .pdf.

Cesari, Jocelyne. 1997. *Être musulman en France aujourd'hui*. Paris: Hachette.

———. 2004. *L'Islam à l'épreuve de l'Occident*. Paris: Éditions La Découverte.

Chilcot, John, et al. 2016. *The Report of the Iraq Inquiry*. London: Her Majesty's Stationery Office, available at http://www.iraqinquiry.org.uk/the-report/.

Clarke, Ronald, and Newman, Greame. 2006. *Outsmarting the Terrorists*. Westport, CT: Praeger Security International.

Clutterbuck, Lindsay. 2014. "Dhiren Barot and Operation Rhyme." In Hoffman and Reinares, 81–100.

Coll, Steve. 2004. *Ghost Wars: The Secret History of the CIA, Afghanistan, and bin Laden, from the Soviet Invasion to September 10, 2001*. New York: Penguin.

References

Cooke, Michael. 2000. *Commanding Right and Forbidding Wrong in Islamic Thought*. Cambridge: Cambridge University Press.

Cour d'appel de Bruxelles. 2004, June 9. Procureur Fédéral c/ Aberkan, Moussaoui, Boulayoun, Sliti, Maaroufi, Aiter, Trabelsi, el-Haddouti and Moulila, Arret de la cour d'appel de Bruxelles, 12e chambre, no. du parquet: FD.21.98.62/03 and FD.35.9859/03.

Crenshaw, Martha, ed. 1995. *Terrorism in Context*. University Park: Pennsylvania State University Press.

Crone, Patricia. 2004. *God's Rule: Government and Islam, Six Centuries of Medieval Islamic Political Thought*. New York: Columbia University Press.

Cronin, Audrey. 2009. *How Terrorism Ends: Understanding the Decline and Demise of Terrorist Campaigns*. Princeton: Princeton University Press.

Cruickshank, Paul, Robertson, Nic, and Shiffman, Ken. 2010, May 15. "American Al Qaeda: The Story of Bryant Neal Vinas." CNN. Available at http://www.cnn.com/SPECIALS/bryant.neal.vinas/index.html.

Della Porta, Donatella. 2013. *Clandestine Political Violence*. New York: Cambridge University Press.

Dhiren Barot and R., 2007, Supreme Court of Judicature, Court of Appeal (Criminal Division), [2007] EWCA Crim 1119, May 16, 2007, available at http://www.bailii.org/cgi-bin/markup.cgi?doc=/ew/cases/EWCA/Crim/2007/1119.html.

Directorate of Terrorist Identities. 2013. "Strategic Accomplishments 2013." Washington, DC: National Counterterrorism Center. Available at https://firstlook.org/theintercept/document/2014/08/05/directorate-terrorist-identities-dti-strategic-accomplishments-2013/.

Elias, Bart, Krouse, William, and Rappaport, Ed. 2005, March 4. "Homeland Security: Air Passenger Prescreening and Counterterrorism." Washington, DC: Congressional Research Center Report for Congress.

Enyo. 2009. *Anatomie d'un Désastre: l'Occident, l'islam et la guerre au XXIe siècle*. Paris: Éditions Denoël.

References

Esposito, John. 1999. *The Islamic Threat: Myth or Reality?* New York: Oxford University Press.

——. 2002. *Unholy War: Terror in the Name of Islam.* New York: Oxford University Press.

Fanon, Frantz. 1961. *Les Damnés de la Terre.* Paris: François Maspero.

Festinger, Leon, Riecken, Henry, and Schachter, Stanley. 1964. *When Prophecy Fails: A Social and Psychological Study of a Modern Group That Predicted the Destruction of the World.* New York: Harper Torchbooks.

Figner, Vera. 1991. *Memoirs of a Revolutionist.* DeKalb: Northern Illinois University Press.

Galanter, Marc. 1990. *Cults: Faith, Healing, and Coercion.* New York: Oxford University Press.

Gambetta, Diego, ed. 2005. *Making Sense of Suicide Missions.* Oxford: Oxford University Press.

Gerges, Fawaz. 2005. *The Far Enemy: Why Jihad Went Global.* Cambridge: Cambridge University Press.

Gilovich, Thomas, Griffin, Dale, and Kahneman, Daniel, eds. 2002. *Heuristics and Biases: The Psychology of Intuitive Judgment.* Cambridge: Cambridge University Press.

Goldhagen, Daniel Jonah. 1996. *Hitler's Willing Executioners: Ordinary Germans and the Holocaust.* New York: Alfred A. Knopf.

Goodwin, Jeff, Jasper, James, and Polletta, Francesca, eds. 2001. *Passionate Politics: Emotions and Social Movements.* Chicago: University of Chicago Press.

Granovetter, Mark. 1973. "The Strength of Weak Ties." *American Journal of Sociology* 78: 1360–80.

——. 1983. "The Strength of Weak Ties: A Network Theory Revisited." *Sociological Theory* 1: 201–33.

——. 1985. "Economic Action and Social Structure: The Problem of Embeddedness." *American Journal of Sociology* 91: 481–510.

Greene, Joshua. 2013. *Moral Tribes: Emotion, Reason, and the Gap between Us and Them.* New York: Penguin.

References

Grigg, Clayton. 2015, May 28. *Ayman Latif et al. v. Eric Holder et al.*, District of Oregon, No. 3:10-CV-00750-BR. Available at https://www.aclu.org/legal-document/latif-et -al-v-holder-et-al-declaration-g-clayton-grigg.

Groen, Janny, and Kranenberg, Annieke. 2010. *Women Warriors for Allah: An Islamist Network in the Netherlands.* Philadelphia: University of Pennsylvania Press.

Gueniffey, Patrice. 2000. *La Politique de la Terreur.* Paris: Gallimard-Collection Tel.

Gunaratna, Rohan. 2002. *Inside al Qaeda: Global Network of Terror.* New York: Columbia University Press.

Gurr, Ted. 1970. *Why Men Rebel.* Princeton: Princeton University Press.

Habeck, Mary. 2006. *Knowing the Enemy: Jihadist Ideology and the War on Terror.* New Haven: Yale University Press.

Hafez, Mohammed. 2003. *Why Muslims Rebel: Repression and Resistance in the Islamic World.* London: Lynne Rienner.

———. 2007. *Suicide Bombers in Iraq: The Strategy and Ideology of Martyrdom.* Washington, DC: United States Institute of Peace Press.

Haidt, Jonathan. 2012. *The Righteous Mind: Why Good People Are Divided by Politics and Religion.* New York: Pantheon.

Haslam, Alexander, Oakes, Penelope, McGarty, Craig, Turner, John, and Onorato, Rina. 1995. "Contextual Changes in the Prototypicality of Extreme and Moderate Outgroup Members." *European Journal of Social Psychology* 25: 509–30.

Haslam, Alexander, and Reicher, Stephen. 2007. "Identity Entrepreneurship and the Consequences of Identity Failure: The Dynamics of Leadership in the BBC Prison Study." *Social Psychology Quarterly* 70, no. 2: 125–47.

———. 2012a. "When Prisoners Take Over the Prison: A Social Psychology of Resistance." *Personality and Social Psychology Review* 16, no. 2: 154–79.

———. 2012b. "Contesting the 'Nature' of Conformity: What Milgram and Zimbardo's Studies Really Show." *Public Library of Science Biology* 10, no. 11: 1–4. Available at http://www.plosbiology.org/article/info%3Adoi%2F10 .1371%2Fjournal.pbio.1001426.

References

Haslam, Alexander, Reicher, Stephen, and Birney, Megan. 2014. "Nothing by Mere Authority: Evidence That in an Experimental Analogue of the Milgram Paradigm Participants Are Motivated Not by Orders but by Appeals to Science." *Journal of Social Issues* 70, no. 3: 473–88.

Haslam, Alexander, Reicher, Stephen, and Platow, Michael. 2011. *The New Psychology of Leadership: Identity, Influence and Power.* Hove, East Sussex: Psychology Press.

Haslam, Alexander, Reicher, Stephen, and Reynolds, Katherine. 2012. "Identity, Influence, and Change: Rediscovering John Turner's Vision for Social Psychology." *British Journal of Social Psychology* 51: 201–18.

Heiberg, Marianne, O'Leary, Brendan, and Tirman, John. 2007. *Terror, Insurgency, and the State: Ending Protracted Conflicts.* Philadelphia: University of Pennsylvania Press.

Hirschman, Albert. 1970. *Exit, Voice, and Loyalty: Responses to Decline in Firms, Organizations, and States.* Cambridge, MA: Harvard University Press.

Hoffer, Eric. 1963. *The True Believer: Thoughts on the Nature of Mass Movements.* New York: Time Incorporated, Time Reading Program Special Edition.

Hoffman, Bruce. 2008, May/June. "The Myth of Grass-Root Terrorism." *Foreign Affairs* 87, no. 3: 133–38.

Hoffman, Bruce, and Reinares, Fernando, eds. 2014. *The Evolution of the Global Terrorist Threat: From 9/11 to Osama bin Laden's Death.* New York: Columbia University Press.

Hogg, Michael, and Reid, Scott. 2006. "Social Identity, Self-Categorization, and the Communication of Group Norms." *Communication Theory* 16: 7–30.

Homeland Security Policy Institute and Critical Incident Analysis Group. 2007. "NETworked Radicalization: A Counter-Strategy." Available at http://www.gwumc.edu/hspi/policy/NETworkedRadicalization.pdf.

Horgan, John. 2005. *The Psychology of Terrorism.* Abingdon, England: Routledge.

Hornsey, Matthew. 2008. "Social Identity Theory and Self-Categorization Theory: A Historical Review." *Social and Personality Psychology Compass* 2, no. 1, 204–22.

References

Ingraham, Barton. 1979. *Political Crime in Europe: A Comparative Study of France, Germany and England.* Berkeley: University of California Press.

Jenkins, Brian. 1977, May. "The Potential for Nuclear Terrorism." *Rand Paper Series.* Santa Monica, CA: RAND Corporation. Available at http://www.rand.org/content/dam/rand/pubs/papers/2006/P5876.pdf.

———. 2010. *Would-Be Warriors: Incidents of Jihadist Terrorist Radicalization in the United States since September 11, 2001.* Santa Monica, CA: RAND Occasional Paper. Available at http://www.rand.org/pubs/occasional_papers/OP292.html.

———. 2011. *Stray Dogs and Virtual Armies: Radicalization and Recruitment to Jihadist Terrorism in the United States since 9/11.* Santa Monica, CA: RAND Occasional Paper. Available at http://www.rand.org/pubs/occasional_papers/OP343.html.

John W. Terry v. Ohio. 392 US 1, 1968.

Jones, Seth, and Libicki, Martin. 2008. *How Terrorist Groups End: Lessons for Countering al Qa'ida.* Santa Monica, CA: RAND Corporation.

Jordan, Javier. 2012. "Analysis of Jihadi Terrorism Incidents in Western Europe, 2001–2010." *Studies in Conflict and Terrorism* 35: 382–404.

———. 2014. "The Foiled Attacks in Italy in 2006." In Hoffman and Reinares, 273–88.

Juzgado Central de Instruccion No. 6, Audiencia Nacional, Madrid, Sumario No 20/2004, 10 abril 2006.

Kahneman, Daniel. 2011. *Thinking, Fast and Slow.* New York: Farrar, Straus, and Giroux.

Kahneman, Daniel, Slovic, Paul, and Tversky, Amos, eds. 1982. *Judgments under Uncertainty: Heuristics and Biases.* Cambridge: Cambridge University Press.

Kahneman, Daniel, and Tversky, Amos, eds. 2000. *Choices, Values and Frames.* Cambridge: Cambridge University Press.

Katz, Elihu, and Lazarsfeld, Paul. 1964. *Personal Influence: The Part Played by People in the Flow of Mass Communications.* New York: Free Press.

References

Keniston, Kenneth. 1968. *Young Radicals: Notes on Committed Youth*. New York: A Harvest Book, Harcourt, Brace, and World.

Kepel, Gilles. 1991. *Les banlieues de l'Islam: Naissance d'une religion en France*. Paris: Éditions du Seuil.

———. 1993. *Muslim Extremism in Egypt: The Prophet and Pharaoh*. Berkeley: University of California Press.

———. 1994. *À l'Ouest d'Allah*. Paris: Éditions du Seuil.

———. 2002. *Jihad: The Trail of Political Islam*. Cambridge, MA: Harvard University Press.

———. 2004. *Fitna: Guerre au coeur de l'islam*. Paris: Éditions Gallimard.

Khosrokhavar, Farhad. 1997. *L'islam des jeunes*. Paris: Flammarion.

———. 2002. *Les nouveaux martyrs d'Allah*. Paris: Flammarion.

———. 2014. *Radicalisation*. Paris: Éditions de la maison des sciences de l'homme.

King, Michael, and Taylor, Donald. 2011. "The Radicalization of Homegrown Jihadists: A Review of Theoretical Models and Social Psychological Evidence." *Terrorism and Political Violence* 23, no. 4: 602–22.

Kirschheimer, Otto. 1961. *Political Justice: The Use of Legal Procedure for Political Ends*. Princeton, NJ: Princeton University Press.

Kittrie, Nicholas, and Wedlock, Eldon, eds. 1998. *The Tree of Liberty: A Documentary History of Rebellion and Political Crime in America*, rev. ed., 2 vols. Baltimore: Johns Hopkins University Press.

Klausen, Jytte. 2010. *Al Qaeda-Affiliated and "Homegrown" Jihadism in the UK: 1999–2010: Research Report*. London: Institute for Strategic Dialogue.

Kruglanski, Arie, Chen, Xiaoyan, Dechesne, Mark, Fishman, Shira, and Orehek, Edward. 2009. "Fully Committed: Suicide Bombers' Motivation and the Quest for Personal Significance." *Political Psychology* 30, no. 3: 331–57.

Lakoff, George. 1987. *Women, Fire, and Dangerous Things: What Categories Reveal about the Mind*. Chicago: University of Chicago Press.

References

Lankford, Adam. 2013. *The Myth of Martyrdom: What Really Drives Suicide Bombers, Rampage Shooters, and Other Self-Destructive Killers.* New York: Palgrave Macmillan.

Le Bon, Gustave. 1895/1998. *Psychologie des foules.* Paris: Quadrige, Presses Universitaires de France.

Lofland, John. 1981. *Doomsday Cult: A Study of Conversion, Proselytization, and Maintenance of Faith.* New York: Irvington.

Lustick, Ian. 2006. *Trapped in the War on Terror.* Philadelphia: University of Pennsylvania Press.

Marques, José, Yzerbyt, Vincent, and Leyens, Jacques-Philippe. 1988. "The 'Black Sheep Effect': Extremity of Judgments toward Ingroup Members as a Function of Group Identification." *European Journal of Social Psychology* 18: 1–16.

Marques, José, Abrams, Dominic, Páez, Dario, and Hogg, Michael. 2003. "Social Categorization, Social Influence, and Rejection of Deviant Group Members." In Hogg and Tindale, 400–424.

Martens, Andy, Sainudiin, Raazesh, Sibley, Chris, Schimel, Jeff, and Webber, David. 2014. "Terrorist Attacks Escalate in Frequency and Fatalities Preceding Highly Lethal Attacks." *PLoS ONE* 9, no. 4: e93732. DOI:10.1371/journal.pone.0093732.

McAdam, Doug. 1982. *Political Process and the Development of Black Insurgency, 1930–1970.* Chicago: University of Chicago Press.

———. 1986, July. "Recruitment to High-Risk Activism: The Case of Freedom Summer." *American Journal of Sociology* 92, no. 1: 64–90.

———. 1988. *Freedom Summer.* New York: Oxford University Press.

McAdam, Doug, Tarrow, Sidney, and Tilly, Charles. 2001. *Dynamics of Contention.* Cambridge: Cambridge University Press.

McCarthy, John, and Zald, Mayer. 1977, May. "Resource Mobilization and Social Movements: A Partial Theory." *American Journal of Sociology* 82, no. 6: 1212–41.

References

McCauley, Clark. 2008 March. "Editor's Welcome to the Inaugural Issue of Dynamics of Asymmetric Conflict." *Dynamics of Asymmetric Conflict* 1, no. 1: 1–5.

McCauley, Clark, and Moskalenko, Sophia. 2011. *Friction: How Radicalization Happens to Them and Us.* New York: Oxford University Press.

McDermott, Terry. 2005. *Perfect Soldiers.* New York: HarperCollins.

McKenna, Joseph. 2012. *The Irish-American Dynamite Campaign: A History, 1881–1896.* Jefferson, NC: McFarland.

Medsger, Betty. 2014. *The Burglary: The Discovery of J. Edgar Hoover's Secret FBI.* New York: Alfred A. Knopf.

Merari, Ariel. 2010. *Driven to Death: Psychological and Social Aspects of Suicide Terrorism.* New York: Oxford University Press.

Michael, George. 2012. *Lone Wolf Terror and the Rise of Leaderless Resistance.* Nashville, TN: Vanderbilt University Press.

Milgram, Stanley. 1974. *Obedience to Authority: An Experimental View.* New York: Harper Torchbooks.

Ministere Public c/ Brigitte et Mir, Tribunal de Grande Instance de Paris, 14eme chambre/2, No d'affaire: 00331139018, Jugement du: 15 Mars 2008.

Ministere Public c/ Daoudi, Beghal, Bounour et autres, Tribunal de Grande Instance de Paris, 10eme chambre/1, No d'affaire: 0125339022, Jugement du: 15 Mars 2005.

Ministere Public c/ Melliti, Bouhalli, Ferchichi et autres, Tribunal de Grande Instance de Paris, 16eme chambre/2, No d'affaire: 0519239028, Jugement du: 23 Octobre 2008.

Moghaddam, Fathali. 2005. "The Staircase to Terrorism: A Psychological Exploration." *American Psychologist* 60, no. 2: 161–69.

———. 2006. *From the Terrorists' Point of View: What They Experience and Why They Come to Destroy.* Westport, CT: Praeger Security International.

Mueller, John. 2006. *Overblown: How Politicians and the Terrorism Industry Inflate National Security Threats and Why We Believe Them.* New York: Free Press.

References

Mueller, John, and Stewart, Mark. 2015. *Chasing Ghosts: The Policing of Terrorism*. New York: Oxford University Press.

National Commission on Terrorist Attacks upon the United States. 2004. *The 9/11 Commission Report, Authorized Edition*. New York: W. W. Norton.

National Counterterrorism Center. 2013. "Watchlisting Guidance." Available at https://firstlook.org/theintercept/document/2014/07/23/march-2013-watchlisting-guidance/.

National Security Division. 2012. "Introduction to National Security Division Statistics on Unsealed International Terrorism and Terrorism-Related Convictions." Washington, DC: US Department of Justice. Available at http://fas.org/irp/agency/doj/doj060612-stats.pdf.

Nesser, Petter. 2008. "Chronology of Jihadism in Western Europe 1994–2007: Planned, Prepared, and Executed Terrorist Attacks." *Studies in Conflict and Terrorism* 31: 924–46.

———. 2010. *Chronology of Jihadism in Western Europe Update 2008–2010*. Kjeller, Norway: Forsvarets forskningsinstitutt (FFI).

———. 2012, January. "Individual Jihadist Operations in Europe: Patterns and Challenges." *CTC Sentinel* 5, no. 1: 15–18.

Nesser, Petter, and Lia, Brynjar. 2010, August. "Lessons Learned from the July 2010 Norwegian Terrorist Plot." *CTC Sentinel* 3, no. 8: 13–17.

Nisbett, Richard, and Cohen, Dov. 1996. *Culture of Honor: The Psychology of Violence in the South*. Boulder, CO: Westview Press.

Oakes, Penelope, Haslam, Alexander, and Turner, John. 1994. *Stereotyping and Social Reality*. Oxford: Blackwell.

Olson, Mancur. 1971. *The Logic of Collective Action: Public Goods and the Theory of Groups*. New York: Schocken Books.

Pantucci, Raffaello. 2010, August. "Manchester, New York and Oslo: Three Centrally Directed al-Qa'ida Plots." *CTC Sentinel* 3, no. 8: 10–13.

References

———. 2011. *A Typology of Lone Wolves: Preliminary Analysis of Lone Islamist Terrorists.* London: The International Centre for the Study of Radicalisation and Political Violence (ICSR), King's College.

———. 2012, July. "A Biography of Rashid Rauf: Al-Qa'ida's British Operative." *CTC Sentinel* 5, no. 7: 12–16.

———. 2015. *"We Love Death as You Love Life": Britain's Suburban Terrorists.* London: Hurt.

Pape, Robert. 2005. *Dying to Win: The Strategic Logic of Suicide Terrorism.* New York: Random House.

Pedahzur, Ami. 2005. *Suicide Terrorism.* Cambridge: Polity Press.

Perry, Simon, and Hasisi, Badi. 2015. "Rational Choice Rewards and the Jihadist Suicide Bomber." *Terrorism and Political Violence* 27: 29–52.

Piehota, Christopher. 2014, September 18. Statement Before the House Homeland Security Committee, Subcommittee on Transportation Security. Washington, DC: Federal Bureau of Investigation. Available at https://www.fbi.gov/news/testimony/tscs-role-in-the-interagency-watchlisting-and-screening-process.

Pinker, Steven. 2011. *The Better Angels of Our Nature: Why Violence Has Declined.* New York: Penguin.

Pisoiu, Daniela. 2012. *Islamist Radicalisation in Europe: An Occupational Change Process.* New York: Routledge.

Post, Jerrold. 2007. *The Mind of the Terrorist: The Psychology of Terrorism from the IRA to al-Qaeda.* New York: Palgrave Macmillan.

Ragin, Charles. 2000. *Fuzzy-Set Social Science.* Chicago: University of Chicago Press.

———. 2008. *Redesigning Social Inquiry: Fuzzy Sets and Beyond.* Chicago: University of Chicago Press.

Ramelsberger, Annette. 2012, July 25. "Al-Qaidas Draht an den Rhein." *Suedeutsche Zeitung* (Munich).

Regina (C'Wealth) v. Elomar & Ors [2010] NSWSC 10 (15 February 2010).

Regina v. Abdulla Ahmed Ali et al., Woolwich Crown Court, 2008.

References

Regina v. Benbrika & Ors (Ruling No. 1) [2011] VSC 76 (11 March 2011).

Regina v. Fattal & Ors [2011] VSC 681 (16 December 2011).

Regina v. Lodhi [2006] NSWSC 691 (23 August 2006).

Regina v. Mohamed Hamid et al., Woolwich Crown Court, 2007 to 2008.

Regina v. Mohammed Shakil et al., Crown Court, Kingston upon Thames, Surrey, Case No: T20087141, 2008.

Regina v. Mohammed Shakil et al., Crown Court, Kingston upon Thames, Surrey, Case No: T20087141, 2009.

Regina v. Momin Khawaja, 2005, Superior Court of Justice, Ottawa, Ontario, Bail Hearing, 2005.

Regina v. Momin Khawaja, 2008, Superior Court of Justice, Ottawa, Ontario, Indictment No. 04-G30282, 2008.

Regina v. Muktar Said Ibrahim et al., Woolwich Crown Court, 2007.

Regina v. Omar Khyam et al., Central Criminal Court, Old Bailey, London, 2006 to 2007.

Regina v. Omar Khyam et al., 2006, "Prepared text of Tuesday's portion of the Crown's opening statement in the trial of seven men alleged to have plotted to bomb London." *Ottawa Citizen*, March 21, 2006, available at http://www.canada.com/ottawacitizen/news/story .html?id=408dc2ed-d950-4ee5-a4b7-392eb5faaf34&k =75162.

Reich, Walter, ed. 1990. *Origins of Terrorism: Psychologies, Ideologies, Theologies, States of Mind.* Washington, DC: Woodrow Wilson Center Press.

Reicher, Stephen. 2003. "The Psychology of Crowd Dynamics." In Hogg and Tindale, 182–208.

Reicher, Stephen, Hopkins, Nick, Levine, Mark, and Rath, Rakshi. 2005, December. "Entrepreneurs of Hate and Entrepreneurs of Solidarity: Social Identity as a Basis for Mass Communication." *International Review of the Red Cross* 87, no. 860: 621–37.

Reicher, Stephen, and Haslam, Alexander. 2006. "Rethinking the Psychology of Tyranny: The BBC Prison Study." *British Journal of Social Psychology* 45: 1–40.

References

Reicher, Stephen, Haslam, Alexander, and Smith, Joanne. 2012. "Working toward the Experimenter: Reconceptualizing Obedience within the Milgram Paradigm as Identification-Based Followership." *Perspectives on Psychological Science* 7, no. 3: 315–24.

Reinares, Fernando. 2010, April–May. "The Madrid Bombings and Global Jihadism." *Survival* 52, no. 2: 83–104.

———. 2014a. "The 2004 Madrid Train Bombings." In Hoffman and Reinares, 29–60.

———. 2014b. "The January 2008 Suicide Bomb Plot in Barcelona." In Hoffman and Reinares, 334–52.

Robertson, Nic, Cruickshank, Paul, and Lister, Tim. 2012a, April 30. "Documents Give New Details on al Qaeda's London Bombings." CNN. Available at http://articles.cnn.com/2012-04-30/world/world_al-qaeda-documents-london-bombings_1_qaeda-s-london-operation-crevice-rashid-rauf?_s=PM:WORLD.

———. 2012b, April 30. "Document Shows Origins of 2006 Plot for Liquid Bombs on Planes." CNN. Available at http://articles.cnn.com/2012-04-30/world/world_al-qaeda-documents_1_qaeda-assad-sarwar-abdulla-ahmed-ali?_s=PM:WORLD.

Rosenmann, Amir, Reese, Gerhard, and Cameron, James. 2016. "Social Identities in a Globalized World: Challenges and Opportunities for Collective Action." *Perspectives on Psychological Science* 11, no. 2: 202–21.

Ross, Lee, and Nisbett, Richard. 1991. *The Person and the Situation: Perspective of Social Psychology*. New York: McGraw-Hill.

Roy, Olivier. 1994. *The Failure of Political Islam*. Cambridge, MA: Harvard University Press.

———. 2004. *Globalized Islam: The Search for a New Ummah*. New York: Columbia University Press.

Sageman, Marc. 2004. *Understanding Terror Networks*. Philadelphia: University of Pennsylvania Press.

———. 2008. *Leaderless Jihad: Terror Networks in the Twenty-First Century*. Philadelphia: University of Pennsylvania Press.

References

———. 2009. "Confronting al-Qaeda: Understanding the Threat in Afghanistan." *Perspectives on Terrorism* 3, no. 4: 4–25.

———. 2010. "Signature Project: Description of Patterned Sequence of Activities Signaling Terrorism." Air Force Research Laboratory, Project Number 13699.018.

———. 2014. "The Stagnation in Terrorism Research." *Terrorism and Political Violence* 26, no. 4: 565–80.

———. 2017 (in press). *The Turn to Political Violence.* Philadelphia: University of Pennsylvania Press.

Scahill, Jeremy, and Devereaux, Ryan. 2014, August 5. "Barack Obama's Secret Terrorist-Tracking System, by the Numbers." *The Intercept.* Available at https://firstlook.org/theintercept/2014/08/05/watch-commander/.

Schmid, Alex. 1984. *Political Terrorism: A Research Guide to Concepts, Theories, Data Bases and Literature.* New Brunswick, NJ: Transaction Books.

Schuurman, Bart, Eijkman, Quirine, and Bakker, Edwin. 2015. "The Hofstadgroup Revisited: Questioning Its Status as a 'Quintessential' Homegrown Jihadist Network." *Terrorism and Political Violence* 27, no. 5: 906–26.

Semelin, Jacques. 2007. *Purify and Destroy: The Political Uses of Massacre and Genocide.* New York: Columbia University Press.

Senate Select Committee on Intelligence. 2012, December 13. "Committee Study of the Central Intelligence Agency's Detention and Interrogation Program: Findings and Conclusions; Executive Summary." Washington, DC: United States Senate. Available at http://www.intelligence.senate.gov/sites/default/files/press/executive-summary_0.pdf.

Silke, Andrew, ed. 2003. *Terrorists, Victims and Society: Psychological Perspectives on Terrorism and Its Consequences.* Chichester, England: John Wiley and Sons.

Silber, Mitchell. 2012. *The Al Qaeda Factor: Plots against the West.* Philadelphia: University of Pennsylvania Press.

References

Silber, Mitchell, and Bhatt, Arvin. 2007. "Radicalization in the West: The Homegrown Threat." New York: New York Police Department Intelligence Division. Available at http://www.nypdshield.org/public/SiteFiles/documents/NYPD_Report-Radicalization_in_the_West.pdf.

Simcox, Robin, Stuart, Hannah, and Ahmed, Houriya. 2010. *Islamist Terrorism: The British Connection.* London: Cromwell Press Group for the Center for Social Cohesion.

Simcox, Robin, and Dyer, Emily. 2013. *Al-Qaeda in the United States: A Complete Analysis of Terrorism Offenses.* London: Henry Jackson Society.

Simon, Jeffrey. 2013. *Lone Wolf Terrorism: Understanding the Growing Threat.* Amherst, NY: Prometheus Books.

Simonson, Peter, ed. 2006, November. "Politics, Social Networks, and the History of Mass Communications Research: Rereading Personal Influence." *Annals of the American Academy of Political and Social Science,* 608.

Sommier, Isabelle. 2008. *La violence politique et son deuil: L'après 68 en France et en Italie.* Rennes: Presses Universitaires de Rennes.

Spears, Russell, and Otten, Sabine. 2012. "Discrimination: Revisiting Tajfel's Minimal Group Studies." In *Social Psychology: Revisiting the Classic Studies,* edited by Joanne Smith and Alexander Haslam. Los Angeles: Sage.

Special Immigration Appeals Commission. 2010, May 18. "Open Judgment: Abid Naseer, Ahmad Faraz Khan, Shoaib Khan, Abdul Wahab Khan and Tariq ur Rehman v. Secretary of State for the Home Department." Appeal no: SC/77/80/81/82/83/09.

Stark, Rodney. 1997. *The Rise of Christianity: How the Obscure, Marginal Jesus Movement became the Dominant Religious Force in the Western World in a Few Centuries.* New York: HarperCollins.

Stark, Rodney, and Bainbridge, William. 1980. "Networks of Faith: Interpersonal Bonds and Recruitment to Cults and Sects." *American Journal of Sociology* 80, no. 6: 1376–95.

References

———. 1985. *The Future of Religion: Secularization, Revival, and Cult Formation*. Berkeley: University of California Press.

———. 1996. *Religion, Deviance, and Social Control*. New York: Routledge.

Stark, Rodney, and Finke, Roger. 2000. *Acts of Faith: Explaining the Human Side of Religion*. Berkeley: University of California Press.

State of Washington v. Naveed Haq, 2009, Superior Court of Washington for King County, No. 06-1-06658-4 SEA.

Steinbach, Michael. 2015, May 28. Declaration of Michael Steinbach, Ayman Latif et al. v. Eric Holder et al., D.OR., no. 3:10-CV-00750-BR. Available at https://www.aclu .org/legal-document/latif-et-al-v-holder-et-al-declaration -michael-steinbach.

Steinberg, Guido. 2013. *German Jihad: On the Internationalization of Islamist Terrorism*. New York: Columbia University Press.

Stone, Geoffrey. 2004. *Perilous Times: Free Speech in Wartime, from the Sedition Act of 1798 to the War on Terrorism*. New York: W. W. Norton.

Stouffer, Samuel, Lumsdaine, Arthur, Lumsdaine, Marion, Williams, Robin, Smith, Brewster, Janis, Irving, Star, Shirley, and Cottrell, Leonard. 1965. *The American Soldier: Combat and Its Aftermath*, vol. 2. New York: Science Editions, John Wiley and Sons.

Taarnby, Michael. 2014. "The Danish Glasvej Case." In Hoffman and Reinares, 312–33.

Tajfel, Henri. 1970. "Experiments in Intergroup Discrimination." *Scientific American* 223: 96–102.

———. 1982. "Social Psychology of Intergroup Relations." *Annual Review of Psychology* 33: 1–39.

Tajfel, Henri, and Turner, John. 1979. "An Integrative Theory of Intergroup Conflict." In *The Social Psychology of Intergroup Relations*, edited by W. G. Austin, and S. Worchel, 33–48. Monterey, CA: Brooks/Cole.

Taylor, Maxwell. 1988. *The Terrorist*. London: Brassey's Defense.

References

Thomas, Jeffrey. 2011. *Background Brief: Global Jihadist Terrorism: Targeting the West.* Washington, DC: Center for the Study of the Presidency and Congress.

Tocqueville, Alexis de. 1986. *De la Démocratie en Amérique; Souvenirs; L'Ancien Régime et la Révolution.* Paris: Bouquins, Éditions Robert Laffont, S.A.

Transportation Security Intelligence Service. 2002 December. "TSA Watch Lists." PowerPoint Presentation, US Department of Transportation, in Rebecca Gordon et al. v. FBI et al., N.D. Cal, no. C 03-01779-CRB. Available at https://www.aclunc.org/sites/default/files/asset_upload_file371_3549.pdf.

Turner, John. 1991. *Social Influence.* Pacific Grove, CA: Brooks/Cole.

———. 1996. "Henri Tajfel: An Introduction." In *Social Groups and Identities: Developing the Legacy of Henri Tajfel*, edited by W. Peter Robinson, 1–23. Oxford: Butterworth-Heinemann.

Turner, John, Hogg, Michel, Oakes, Penelope, Reicher, Stephen, and Wetherell, Margaret. 1987. *Rediscovering the Social Group: A Self-Categorization Theory.* Oxford: Blackwell.

Turner, John, Oales, Penelope, Haslam, Alexander, and McGarty, Craig. 1994, October. "Self and Collective: Cognition and Social Context." *Personality and Social Psychology Bulletin* 20, no. 5: 454–63.

U.S. Department of Defense. 2007a. *Verbatim Transcripts of Combatant Status Review Tribunal Hearings for ISN 10017 (Abu Faraj al Libi).*

———. 2007b. *Verbatim Transcripts of Combatant Status Review Tribunal Hearings for ISN 10024 (Khalid Shaykh Muhammad).*

———. 2007c. Biographical information on Abd al-Hadi al-Iraqi, April 27, 2007, available at http://www.defense.gov/news/Apr2007/d20070427hvd.pdf.

———. 2008. *JTF-GTMO Detainee Assessment ISN 10017 (Abu Faraj al Libi)*, September 10, 2008, available at https://wikileaks.org/gitmo/prisoner/10017.html.

References

U.S. v. Abdal Hadi al Iraqi. 2014. U.S. Department of Defense, MC Form 458, Continuation of the Charges and Specifications, Receipt by Convening Authority, February 10, 2014.

U.S. v. Adis Medunjanin. 2012. Eastern District of New York, No. 10-CR-19 (JG).

U.S. v. Faisal Shahzad. 2010. Southern District of New York, No. 10-CR-541 (MGC), Government's Memorandum in Connection with the Sentencing of Faisal Shahzad, September 29, 2010.

U.S. v. John Doe [Bryant Neal Vinas]. 2009. U.S. District Court, Eastern District of New York, No. 08-CR-823 [NGG] (Sealed).

U.S. v. Mohamed Osman Mohamud. 2013. District of Oregon, No. 3:10-CR-475-KI.

U.S. v. Mustafa Kamel Mustafa. 2014. Southern District of New York, No. 04-CR-356 (KBF).

U.S. v. Sulaiman abu Gaith. 2014. Southern District of New York, No. S13-98-CR-1028 (LAK).

U.S. v. Tahawwur Rana. 2011. Northern District of Illinois, Eastern Division, Docket No. 09 CR 830 (HDL).

van Stekelenburg, Jacquelien. 2013. "The Social Psychology or Protest." *Current Sociology Review* 61, no. 5–6: 886–905.

———. 2014. "Going All the Way: Politicizing, Polarizing, and Radicalizing Identity Offline and Online." *Sociology Compass* 8, no. 5: 540–55.

van Stekelenburg, Jacquelien, and Klandermans, Bert. 2007. "Individuals in Movements: A Social Psychology of Contention." In *Handbook of Social Movements Across Disciplines,* edited by Bert Klandermans and Conny Roggeband, 157–204. New York: Springer Science + Business Media.

Vidino, Lorenzo. 2014. *Home-Grown Jihadism in Italy: Birth, Development and Radicalization Dynamics.* Brussels: European Foundation for Democracy.

Weaver, Ray. 2012a, May 3. "Prosecution Rests Case in Terror Trial." *The Copenhagen Post Online.* Available at http://cphpost.dk/news/national/prosecution-rests-case-terror-trial.

References

———. 2012b, June 4. "Terror Suspects Guilty in Planned Jyllands-Posten Attack." *The Copenhagen Post Online.* Available at http://cphpost.dk/news/national/terror -suspects-guilty-planned-jyllands-posten-attack.

Whelehan, Niall. 2012. *The Dynamiters: Irish Nationalism and Political Violence in the Wider World, 1867–1900.* Cambridge: Cambridge University Press.

White, Jenny. 2002. *Islamist Mobilization in Turkey: A Study in Vernacular Politics.* Seattle: University of Washington Press.

Wickham, Carrie Rosefsky. 2002. *Mobilizing Islam: Religion, Activism and Political Change in Egypt.* New York: Columbia University Press.

Wiktorowicz, Quintan. 2001. *The Management of Islamic Activism: Salafis, the Muslim Brotherhood, and State Power in Jordan.* Albany: State University of New York Press.

———, ed. 2004. *Islamic Activism: A Social Movement Theory Approach.* Bloomington: Indiana University Press.

———. 2005. *Radical Islam Rising: Muslim Extremism in the West.* Oxford: Rowman and Littlefield.

Wilson, Kelly. 2011, July 8. "Homegrown Violent Extremism: Identifying Highly Diagnostic and First Amendment-Conscious Indicators." Washington, DC: Washington Regional Threat and Analysis Center, the Metropolitan Police Department.

Wright, Lawrence. 2006. *The Looming Tower: Al-Qaeda and the Road to 9/11.* New York: Alfred A. Knopf.

Zimbardo, Philip. 2007. *The Lucifer Effect: Understanding How Good People Turn Evil.* New York: Random House.

Acknowledgments

Any book is a team effort. I would like to thank Mitch Silber, with whom I started exploring some of this book's arguments a long time ago. Peter Agree from the University of Pennsylvania Press encouraged me to write them down, and Noreen O'Connor-Abel coordinated the editing of Robert Milks and Megan Bailey with her usual professionalism. I would also like to thank Rafe Sagalyn for negotiating the contract with the press. My greatest thanks go to my wife, Jody, who was always there for me, ready to discuss my ideas and editing the various drafts of the book. Without all of them, this book would not have been possible.